GOVERNING THE MILITARY

A military is the most significant tool of a nation's foreign policy, and (hopefully) the tool of last resort. Yet the control a civilian leader has over the military is, in many respects, an encumbered and fractured control. The military's organizational culture, role in society, size, and considerable autonomy are potential obstacles to true civilian control over the military, even in peacetime. A brief but historically informed text intended for students of the presidency or national security, *Governing the Military* addresses the gamut of challenges a new U.S. President faces as commander-in-chief.

Andrew L. Stigler is Associate Professor of National Security Affairs at the United States Naval War College.

Presidential Briefings

Series Editor: Robert J. Spitzer,
State University of New York College at Cortland

The **Presidential Briefings** series provides concise and readable introductions to topics of concern to those who have been and will be President of the United States. For students of the presidency, these books provide a highly practical and accessible overview of an important subject related to the presidency. By approaching their subjects from the vantage point of what a president needs to know, and what the citizenry need to know about the presidency, these books are authoritative and significant works.

Robert J. Spitzer is Distinguished Service Professor and Chair of the Political Science Department at the State University of New York College at Cortland, as well as Visiting Professor at Cornell University. He led the Presidents and Executive Politics Organization (formerly the Presidency Research Group) of the American Political Science Association from 2001–03, and he is a regular contributor to various media outlets.

Governing the Military
Andrew L. Stigler

Presidential Relations with Congress
Richard S. Conley

For more information about this series, please visit www.routledge.com/Presidential-Briefings-Series/book-series/PBSTRANS

GOVERNING THE MILITARY

Andrew L. Stigler

Routledge
Taylor & Francis Group

NEW YORK AND LONDON

First published 2019
by Routledge
711 Third Avenue, New York, NY 10017

and by Routledge
2 Park Square, Milton Park, Abingdon, Oxon, OX14 4RN

Routledge is an imprint of the Taylor & Francis Group, an informa business

Library of Congress Cataloging-in-Publication Data
A catalog record for this book has been requested

DISCLAIMER: The views expressed are solely those of the author,
and should not be attributed to any U.S. Government department
or agency.

ISBN: 978-1-138-48977-6 (hbk)
ISBN: 978-1-138-48978-3 (pbk)
ISBN: 978-1-351-03678-8 (ebk)

Typeset in Bembo
by Apex CoVantage, LLC

For
Stephen and Virginia Stigler
with love and gratitude

CONTENTS

PREFACE

One of the tremendous advantages of teaching at the Naval War College has been the opportunity to become acquainted with a wide array of officers from all four services, as well as civilian national security officials—individuals possessing a great diversity of experiences, perspectives, and expertise. Of the countless interactions I have had with war college students and colleagues over more than a decade, one is of particular relevance for this book. As one might imagine, following a presidential election that designates a new chief executive, the Pentagon prepares a series of briefings for the incoming occupant of the oval office. These briefings cover a wide range of topics—the United States' defensive capabilities, the capabilities and disposition of adversaries, the status of ongoing operations, and anything else the nation's most senior uniformed leadership believes the new president needs to know.

My student was involved in this series of briefings, and was present while the president-elect received a well-prepared avalanche of information. What he most vividly remembered from the episode was that the president-elect uttered a single phrase with considerable frequency: "I had no idea."

The president-elect's surprise should come as no surprise. It has been expected since the nation's founding that the president would need to maintain a level of secrecy in international affairs, even from cabinet members and the vice president. Shortly after taking office, George Washington asked for a "secret service fund" in his first message to Congress. He was soon granted his request, a fund to conduct clandestine operations without Congressional oversight.

Even in wartime, presidents left close advisors uninformed about important programs and developments. Harry Truman, when he assumed the presidency following the death of Franklin Roosevelt, discovered he had been completely uninformed about a range of wartime programs—including the United States' effort to develop the world's first atomic bomb.

Presidents-elect are forced to simultaneously familiarize themselves with a vast ocean of information at the same time that they take the reins of one of the world's largest bureaucracies. Though we speak of civilian control of the military in the United States (and the phrase is by and large an accurate one), it is also true that the military bureaucracy and officer corps have their own perspectives on what measures are necessary to secure the nation, and avenues through which to express those perspectives when they differ with those of the president. The military also has a broad and solid base of support in the country. These factors can conspire to complicate and even frustrate a president's efforts to shape or utilize the military instrument of power.

This book addresses the most important issues that can confront a president seeking to steer the military's course in the domestic and international arenas, issues that informed citizens need to understand as well. The framers of the Constitution left to the citizens of the new American democracy the task of evaluating, through elections, the tenure of president. What perhaps receives too little attention is the fact that arriving at a well-cast vote is a decision best based on sound knowledge of the chief executive's powers and responsibilities. Given the wide latitude a president enjoys in the execution of his or her commander-in-chief responsibilities, there is considerable room to argue that the president's national security role should be of primary concern when casting a ballot. "It's foreign policy, stupid," might be a more accurate recasting of a former president's campaign slogan, at least from the standpoint of what a president genuinely controls. This book offers an exploration of the range of considerations that a president faces as he or she prepares to govern the military.

ACKNOWLEDGMENTS

The first acknowledgments must go to Christopher Fettweis at Tulane University and Bob Spitzer at SUNY-Cortland. Chris provided me with the initial opportunity to contribute to the series, and Bob has been highly supportive of the project as it approached completion. I am deeply grateful to them both.

Some of my war college colleagues have been particularly generous in their willingness to offer insights from either their experience in government or the military. John Cloud has always been willing to offer insight from his experience as a former Ambassador and NSC official. Jon Myers provided experience from his multiple tours as an Army infantry officer in Iraq that lent insight to my understanding of Iraq's reconstruction. Steve Knott's deep knowledge of the presidency has informed my understanding of the institution over the years.

Other colleagues also provided insights or recommended works at specific junctures, including David Burbach, John Maurer, and Rick Norton. Countless Naval War College students have offered insights that have informed what follows.

The library staff at the Naval War College has offered tremendous assistance over the years, and this project was no exception. I was informed some time ago that I was the Naval War College inter-library loan system's "best customer," which was not intended as an admonishment, but which I took on board as a caveat. The entire library staff has my gratitude. I thank Heidi

Garcia, Robin Lima, and Jack Miranda in particular for their tireless and enthusiastic assistance.

Taylor & Francis has been generous in their support of this project, and it is a privilege to offer this contribution to the series. Jennifer Knerr and Ze'ev Sudry were understanding of delays, offered valuable advice, and made the transition of the series from another publishing house as smooth as possible.

The views expressed in this work are solely those of the author, and in no way reflect the views of the Department of Defense, the U.S. Navy, or any other U.S. Government department or agency.

Andrew L. Stigler
Newport, Rhode Island

INTRODUCTION

Every four years, the American electorate selects someone to take on an impossible job.

The U.S. Department of Defense is among the largest bureaucracies in the world. Employing over two million service members and civilian personnel, it is the largest employer in the United States. Simply managing the organization is a vastly complex task. However, a president must also decide when, and in what manner, to deploy or not to deploy American military power around the globe. Presidents are served by thousands of dedicated individuals in this four-year task. But the most significant decisions regarding the military are the president's alone. And while it can be easy to exaggerate global instability, it is always possible that a president may face a situation in which the lives of millions hang in the balance.

In theory, the president—as head of the Executive Branch of the U.S. Government—has near-total control over the priorities, personnel, and overseas deployment of the U.S. military. If the president commands the Department of Defense to take on a new priority or a new mission (short of major war and subject to Congressional funding restrictions), that presidential order should, in theory, be carried out. Officers in the military serve at the president's discretion, and even four-star generals and admirals can be fired at any time.

However, the reality that faces an incoming president is considerably more complicated. The military has an independent base of support in the United States, and there are many ways in which the military can insulate itself from political influence. The nation's military leaders are those best positioned to influence military recruitment and promotions, and the department plays a major role in recommending candidates for the nation's highest military positions. Organizational behavior can create unexpected behavioral proclivities, resisting a commander-in-chief's instructions. It can be very difficult to influence a large, insulated bureaucracy that has a measure of independent political support—even if that organization is nominally under a president's complete control. Strategies for stalling and neutralizing unwanted change are well understood by the sophisticated civilians and military officers working for the department.

This is not to say that these national security professionals, both civilians and serving military, are not patriotic and observant of their role in government. But policy inertia and organizational culture can be powerful forces. Organizations often resist change. Those currently serving in the organization have often prospered by cultivating the status quo, and they are the individuals most familiar with the arguments for keeping things as they are.

Presidents have not always been well served by military advice. Consider the Cuban Missile Crisis, a time when the potential for a catastrophic conflict seemed particularly apparent. During those tense days in October 1962, President John F. Kennedy's most senior uniformed advisor, Chairman of the Joint Chiefs of Staff Maxwell Taylor, offered arguments in favor of a sudden military strike: a days-long air campaign, followed by a blockade and possible invasion. Taylor recommended that the Cubans and the Soviets be offered no warning, which meant no time whatsoever for diplomacy. "We're impressed, Mr. President, with the great importance of getting a strike with all the benefit of surprise," Taylor said on October 16.

Had Kennedy been more easily convinced by Taylor's arguments, or more easily swayed by stark words spoken by men with stars on their shoulders, the outcome of the Cuban Missile Crisis would have been quite different. Kennedy himself estimated that the likelihood of general war with the Soviet Union was "between one in three and even." He could well have unintentionally exaggerated the risk of war with the Soviets. Leaders involved in high-stakes crisis negotiations are often not the best estimators of the actual threat posed by a particular situation. But given the starkness of the outcome being contemplated—a potential nuclear exchange—one cannot help but have one's attention arrested by the president's assessment.

It may be worth contemplating that a prior foreign policy initiative of the Kennedy administration—the disastrous invasion of the Bay of Pigs in April 1961—may have been a debacle with fortuitous timing. At that time, Kennedy had been recently installed in the oval office and inherited a plan from the administration of Dwight Eisenhower that was at an advanced stage of preparation. Kennedy gave the go-ahead, and the Cuban expatriates made an amphibious landing on one of the island's beaches—and were quickly killed or rounded up. The invasion was a major embarrassment for the United States. Yet if Kennedy's experience with the Bay of Pigs caused him to hesitate to rely on advice from his most senior officers during the Cuban Missile Crisis, then the Bay of Pigs invasion may have been, in retrospect, a most fortunate disaster.

This book is an effort to explore the issues that face an incoming president as he or she prepares to take control of the largest, most cumbersome, most powerful, most expensive, and most critical element of the Executive Branch of government: the United States military. This volume will investigate the spectrum of considerations that a president will need to grasp in order to govern this institutional behemoth. Rather than rely on experimentation to prepare a chief executive for this critical national security role (as Kennedy did, inadvertently), this work will seek to impart some of the lessons of history.

It should be emphasized at the outset that this book does not seek to provide an evenhanded account of the military's role in American society, or to assess the many contributions that the military makes—sometimes at grievous cost of human life—to the national security of the United States. These dimensions of the military's role are discussed elsewhere. Instead, this is an attempt to ferret out the potential problems and challenges a president might encounter as an executive in charge of a vast, complicated, and semi-independent organization. Just as an automobile manual focuses on a car's controls and warning indicators (while eschewing celebration of the joys of driving and the technical achievement of mechanized mobility), this book takes a similar approach to the military.

Chapter 1 explores the intersection of the military and American society, as well as Congress's critical role in the development and support of the institution of the military. Congress has great power to affect the organization of the military through legislation, and everything the military owns is funded by Congress. These facts can greatly constrain a president's ability to shape the military. Other aspects of presidential control are almost never affected by Congress, such as major military deployments and limited military actions. In addition, the military's unique role in U.S. society, and the respect it generates, can impinge or aid presidential control. Secretary Robert Gates warned in 2011 that military personnel costs are "eating us alive," pointing to an area of the budget where social and Congressional support for the military can sharply limit the president's ability to make changes. This chapter includes a discussion of the budgetary and procurement processes.

Chapter 2 investigates the task of changing the military as an organization, and the challenge of long-term strategic planning. When presidents attempt to affect change in the military, a wide array of obstacles can impose themselves. Bureaucratic intractability, as well as appeals for Congressional resistance, can impinge on a president's latitude in this area. The military also plays a significant role in strategic planning, and in generating strategic documents such as the National Military Strategy. The military can, at times, resist presidential initiatives. For example, President Barack Obama believed that General Stanley McChrystal and others in the Department of Defense attempted to shape the domestic political environment in which Obama deliberated the future Afghanistan strategy in 2009.

Given that irregular counterterrorism activity appears highly likely to be a staple of U.S. national security policy for the foreseeable future, Chapter 3 explores the challenges inherent in counterterrorism activity, with a focus on the use of drones. The military's increasing investment in unmanned aircraft technology will make use of this rapidly evolving weapons platform both politically palatable and (for the United States) casualty-free. Obama's significant increase in the number of drone strikes during his presidency may be a harbinger of what is to come. Given that strike orders must often be given with little warning, the president must, at times, place considerable latitude in the hands of local commanders. This chapter looks at the complexities and issues that are likely to arise in presidential control—or, at times, the lack of presidential control—over such actions.

Chapter 4 explores the impact of a crisis. In a national security emergency, the President is heavily reliant on the military for advice, preparatory actions, and support for diplomatic efforts. When time is limited or there is a pressing need for decisions and information, the president must be alert to the possibility of organizational behavior affecting any or all aspects of the military's role. Deployment decisions, which are common in crises, can also have a dramatic impact on both policy debates and international events. Military preparations can send inadvertent signals to adversaries, unnecessarily raising the risk of conflict.

Chapter 5 addresses the decision to go to war, the ultimate test of presidential leadership in the national-security realm. Presidents have wide and near-total latitude in their role as commander-in-chief; greater control, in fact, than any other aspect of presidential control of the military. Abraham Lincoln fired seven generals-in-chief during the Civil War—an act that would be seen as a monumental indication of uncertain leadership today—and he was still afforded the latitude to pursue the war to victory, even winning re-election in 1864. When deciding whether to take the nation to war, presidents are simultaneously dependent on the military for advice and reliant upon them to execute commands. For some officers, their belief in the military's superior experience and knowledge can influence policymaking during a prelude to war. Yet, as Eliot Cohen argues in his book *Supreme Command*, presidents can sometimes override military preferences to the benefit of the overall war effort. This chapter explores these presidential powers and their limitations.

"No battle plan survives contact with the enemy." Helmuth von Moltke's words point to the need to be able to change strategy in mid-conflict, and Chapter 6 addresses this challenge. Raising the prospect of a change in strategy can open a president to political criticism, and it can lead to a host of actors attempting to sway the president in one direction or another. President Truman's decision to fire General MacArthur during the Korean conflict is a prominent example of the tensions that can arise when a president disagrees with senior commanders. Truman's move was widely criticized at the time, but the verdict of history has endorsed his drastic measure as a necessary assertion of civilian control of the military. Presidents may seek a strategy change during wartime, but organizational inertia can lead to institutional resistance from the military. This chapter examines these concerns.

For some wars, victory is only the beginning of the military's work, and Chapter 7 explores the postwar challenge of social reconstruction. World War II, as well as the conflicts in Afghanistan and Iraq, demonstrate that the military often plays a role in long-term postwar reconstruction efforts. Though some civilian leaders may envision a quick exit—as Secretary Donald Rumsfeld did after the invasion of Iraq in 2003—social deterioration and strategic considerations can mitigate powerfully against such desires. This chapter will particularly focus on the serious and potentially insuperable shortcomings the military faces in reconstruction efforts commanded by the president—paucities of expertise in linguistics, in cultural insight, and other essential skills.

At the outset of this presidential briefing, it is worth considering the extent to which the United States may have been very fortunate in the selection of its early presidents, particularly George Washington. Washington respected the limits and responsibilities of his role in the new republic, and most importantly he sought to chart a path of humility and responsibility in power that he hoped would influence future presidents. As Byron Daynes puts it, "he appeared uncomfortable in possession of power, wished to remain out of the focus of attention, and did not seek position." He was perhaps the perfect first executive for a nation—respected, capable, and industrious, but also highly cognizant of the need to set a model of peaceful and conflict-free executive transition in a young democracy.

Presidents can arrive in office with little or no experience in military affairs, and with little or no understanding of the military as an organization. Indeed, some presidents, such as Lyndon Johnson, hoped to avoid deep involvement in international affairs and focus instead on domestic matters. But the course of human events does not bend to the preferences of any one executive. George W. Bush campaigned against "nation-building" in the 2000 campaign, and yet found himself engaged in two vast and complex nation-building enterprises in Afghanistan and Iraq. Barack Obama believed it was time for America to extract itself from Iraq, and found that the increased threat posed by ISIS compelled a partial reversal.

It is difficult to overstate the scope of the military as an ongoing industrial enterprise. The purchase of weapons platforms (some of which are collections of untested and expensive technologies) is a daunting but necessary exercise. As of this writing, the first aircraft carrier in the new Ford class, CV-78, is projected by the Government Accountability Office to ultimately cost $12.9 billion, and that figure is likely to increase. Though many thousands of experts aid the occupant of the oval office, the president ultimately decides which weapons the Department of Defense will ask Congress to fund. For both citizens of the United States and interested observers, possessing a grasp of the complexities involved in managing and directing the world's largest military can shed light on what otherwise might seem to be opaque or puzzling presidential decisions.

Presidents may have the opportunity to decide what issues they will address during their term in office. At other times, decisions and crises will be forced upon the chief executive by world events, and while these may be mitigated, they often cannot be ignored. Ted Sorenson, a senior advisor to John F. Kennedy, argued that

> The fundamental nature of the White House makes it inevitable that vital decisions, either many or few, will be made . . . and that the same basic forces and factors will repeatedly shape those decisions. . . . A President may ignore these forces or factors—he may even be unaware of them—but he cannot escape them. He may choose to decide in solitude, but he does not decide in a vacuum.[1]

Note

1 Theodore C. Sorenson, *Decision-Making in the White House: The Olive Branch or the Arrows* (New York: Columbia University Press, 1963), p. 7.

1

THE MILITARY'S ROLE
Society and Congress

There are many reasons for the prominence of the military in American society and political culture. Our national myth is one that has been formed around violence and resistance—violence for a purpose, but violence nonetheless. Over the past century, it is military conflict that has defined the turning points of history. Struggles against Nazi Germany, Imperial Japan, and terrorism have played a critical role in defining the nation. The Americans who fought in World War II have been called "the Greatest Generation," not for any political improvements that came about during this time, but for the violent struggle through which they persevered.

In almost every recent poll on the United States population's view of United States government departments and agencies, the American military is the most popular part of the U.S. government—usually by a long shot. A 2016 Gallup poll found that 72% of Americans have "a great deal" or "quite a lot" of confidence in the military, more than any other institution. In this poll, the military scored highest of all institutions mentioned in the survey—higher than the police, the church, and the medical system. The military's poll numbers remained consistently high even through the most pessimistic years of the occupation of Iraq (2004–07). Many Americans consider those in uniform to be the nation's finest and bravest, willing to be sent into harm's way at a moment's notice, obeying every order, and sacrificing all when the nation's security requires it.

Furthermore, the U.S. military is perceived as a largely apolitical organization, even though it is not. While the military does not have an overt leaning toward one of the two parties, senior officers certainly recognize that they are part of a political system, and usually act accordingly. Generals and admirals are often promoted based on their political skills, and on their ability to both manage political relationships and curry favor on Capitol Hill. Chairman of the Joint Chiefs of Staff General Colin Powell was regularly extolled with phrases such as "a great statesman and diplomat" even before he took off the uniform. This quote illustrates the perception that, for many, the military is an exclusive vocation, while diplomacy and statesmanship are not—even accomplished and skilled wartime presidents, such as Franklin Roosevelt, would never be extolled as a "great general."

In contrast with the military, the presidency is seen as a political position, and recent presidents have rarely garnered approval ratings in excess of 60% (George W. Bush, in the immediate aftermath of 9/11, was among the rare exceptions). Since presidents are more transparently part of the political process, they are more likely to become associated with the political struggles of the day. Even George Washington was occasionally pilloried in his time. After issuing his Neutrality Proclamation in 1783 asserting that the United States would remain unaligned in the war between Britain and France, John Adams wrote, "Ten thousand people in the streets of Philadelphia, day after day, threatened to drag Washington out of his house and effect a revolution in the government."

Extolling the qualities of the military is virtually a prerequisite for those seeking political office. But if the primary goal of a government is effective governance, respect for the military is not always a good thing. Insofar as it influences presidential control of the military, the elevated status of the military in U.S. society can both raise obstacles to presidential command and create governmental proclivities. Although the president is the commander-in-chief, both in theory and in fact, the occupant of the oval office takes a risk when he or she is seen as opposing the preferences and needs of the military. Even the appearance of seeming insufficiently attentive to the well-being of the troops can be costly.

In December 2004, then-Secretary of Defense Donald Rumsfeld was on a tour of Iraq and held a question and answer session with a group of service personnel. Answering a query from an Army specialist who spoke of how he and his comrades scrounged in scrap heaps for metal that could be used to increase the armor of their Humvees, Rumsfeld observed, "You go to war with the army you have, not the army you might want or wish to have at a later time."

While Rumsfeld was criticized for the remark, it is factually correct. When it was designed, the Humvee was expected to be used as a transport vehicle behind an established front line in an engagement with the organized militaries of the Warsaw Pact, It was not conceived as a vehicle that would be targeted by improvised explosives. Crises and conflicts do not wait patiently while the military procurement process generates the perfect mix of equipment and capabilities for a given situation.

Rumsfeld was pilloried for the statement because it gave an appearance of executive indifference to the needs of the soldier on the ground. Conservative commentator William Kristol, in an essay titled "The Defense Secretary We Have," called Rumsfeld's remark "arrogant buck-passing." Rumsfeld titled one of the chapters in his memoir dealing with the occupation of Iraq "Catastrophic Success," and notes that he argued at the time: "We need to understand our limitations. . . . There are some things the U.S. simply cannot accomplish." These limitations became all too apparent over the years that followed.

In the same vein, concern over military casualties has had a profound impact on military strategy at times. During Operation Allied Force—the 1999 air campaign over Kosovo—the U.S. military flew missions at altitudes that would bring the risk of being shot down by a surface-to-air missile to the absolute minimum. As a consequence, the air campaign was conducted with less accuracy and less aggressiveness than might have otherwise been achieved, and some missions were aborted when the risk posed by Yugoslavia's air defenses was judged to be too great.

In a telling example of casualty sensitivity from that same conflict, President Bill Clinton declined to send Apache helicopters into combat, even though the Apaches had been sent to the region after the air campaign began in order to buttress the coalition's firepower. The helicopters, collectively known as Task Force Hawk, had been brought to the Balkans at considerable expense: the deployment was estimated to have cost $500 million, as much as a quarter of the total bill for Operation Allied Force. Ultimately, however, concern over possible losses led to the decision not to employ the Apaches.

It is hard to predict when casualties will alter a society's view of a conflict. Unlike parliamentary systems of government, presidents are not at risk of being thrown out of office at a moment's notice by a vote of no-confidence. Presidents often have considerable latitude to ignore high casualty rates, and public opinion, during a lengthy conflict. President George W. Bush mentioned a number of times during his exit interviews that he was proud of the fact that he did not bend with every change in public opinion. Prior to the 2006 midterm elections, when his advisors recommended that he improve his poll numbers by bringing some troops home from Iraq, he declined. "I made it clear I would set troop levels to achieve victory in Iraq, not victory at the polls," he wrote afterwards.

There is a tendency to assume that insulating a president from negative public opinion is always detrimental. This is not the case. Bush's resistance to public opinion paved the way for the Iraq surge and a shift in U.S. counterinsurgency strategy, two innovations that contributed to a dramatic downturn in the level of violence in Iraq. Both Hillary Clinton and Barack Obama were senators in 2007 when the decision to engage in the surge was undertaken; both later conceded that it had been successful. In this case, the insulation from society that a president enjoys arguably led to an opportunity to improve the course of events.

Not all examples of presidents ignoring public opinion turn out well. The Vietnam War would be a conflict in this latter category, in which the presidential insulation enjoyed by Johnson and Nixon allowed a failing war effort to continue, even in the face of one of the most strident anti-war movements in history. By August 1968, a slight majority of Americans (53%) believed that the decision to send large numbers of troops to South Vietnam had been a mistake. An anti-war protest on 15 November 1969 drew as many as half a million participants. Despite the war's unpopularity, the doomed effort to support South Vietnam continued for years. Once Congress has authorized an initial use of force, and absent a Congressional effort to defund an operation, presidents can independently determine when they wish to be influenced by society in their ability to wage a war.

Congress and the Military Instrument of Power

In David Mayhew's book *Divided We Govern*, he argued that presidential leadership regarding Congress "has three necessary components: an agenda, will, and skill."[1] Presidential agendas, the first of Mayhew's components, can be expansive or limited—the degree to which a president can control the agenda depends on what opportunities he or she is afforded. The second component, will, refers to the extent to which a president is determined to see something through Congress; Lyndon Johnson was famous for aggressively lobbying his former colleagues on the Hill. And skill was broadly conceived by Mayhew as political skill—understanding Congress's processes and people, as well as having good timing, adroit public relations, and persuasive capabilities.

Note that power does not fit well into Mayhew's trio of components. A president has no controlling power, or at least none over Congress without the consent of a portion of that body. Sometimes, having influence with even just a few Congressmen can lead to a limited result that can have a political impact, such as the introduction of a piece of legislation. But the intersection of the executive and legislative branches of government is where the Constitution imposes a particularly potent separation of powers.

In at least one respect, Congress offers a perfect contrast to the U.S. military: whereas the military is durably popular, the public's opinion of Congress is usually quite low. Since 2010, Gallup's poll of the U.S. public's approval of Congress has usually been in the teens. In November 2013, Congress's approval level broke the single-digit barrier and reached 9%. Why is this? Americans registering disapproval of Congress do not hate their country, for the most part. Moreover, members of both the Senate and the House of Representatives tend to have re-election rates in excess of 80%, even topping 90% in some elections.

Part of the explanation for such low approval ratings likely lies with the media. Congress tends to get media attention when something is unresolved—and, rightly or no, Congress tends to get the blame for any lack of political progress, even when the institution itself is not at fault.

In addition, these are unusually partisan times. A 2016 Pew study found that the number of American citizens who have an "unfavorable" view of the other party is at a record high—91% of Republican responders responded they thought unfavorably of the other party, as did 86% of Democrats. Since the minority party in Congress can sometimes have the power to block legislation proposed by the majority (usually in the Senate), some of this partisan rancor is bound to have an impact on Congress's ability to get things done.

Another factor contributing to Congress's unpopularity is likely Congress's institutional design. Congress is designed to approach new legislation slowly and deliberately, and hopefully prevent the passage of bad laws. It is not designed to speed through laws, even excellent ones. Congress can move quickly when there is near-unanimity—witness the authorization for the use of force against those responsible for the 9/11 attacks, passed on 14 September 2001. But a system designed to be laborious is bound to frustrate many of the citizens of the republic that the system serves.

There are three key ways that Congress influences the military, including presidential control of the military. The first is the power to make war. The Constitution specifically allots the power to "declare" war to Congress. This was, in part, an attempt to prevent the institution of the Presidency from mirroring the British monarchy. The original signers of the Declaration of Independence had literally rebelled against the idea that the responsibility for determining issues of war and peace should be vested in a single individual, be that individual a monarch or a president. Congress's ability to impact issues of war and peace will be discussed in a later chapter.

The second critical area in which Congress plays a role is in the structure of the military. It is through legislation that the organizational structure and hierarchy of the military are determined. And third, the power of the purse gives Congress dominant control over military acquisition. The two latter areas of Congressional influence on the military are discussed in the remainder of this chapter.

Organization and Structure of the Military

It is true that the president has the latitude to alter the military's organization on the fly, particularly during the course of a conflict. But the foundational elements of the structure of the military are laid out in U.S. code, which means fundamental changes to the Department of Defense involve legislative changes. In particular, two post-World War II acts of legislation have had a dramatic impact on the structure of today's military: the National Security Act of 1947 and the Goldwater-Nichols Act of 1986.

During World War II, the military was a markedly different organization. The massive land-based air forces the U.S. contributed to campaigns in Europe and in the Pacific were actually part of the Army—the U.S. Army Air Corps. The Department of War constituted only the U.S. Army; the U.S. Navy was entirely separate, operated by the Department of the Navy. There was no National Security Council.

The broad structure of today's U.S. military is largely based on the National Security Act of 1947, a vast reorganization of the military based on the lessons learned from World War II. The Air Force was made a separate service within the Department of the Air Force. The Department of War was renamed the Department of the Army. The three independent services (Army, Navy, Air Force), each with their own departments and civilian service secretaries, were consolidated into the National Military Establishment—later renamed the Department of Defense. The Marine Corps, threatened with declining budgets and dissolution following World War II, was preserved in U.S. Code as a separate service, though within the Department of the Navy. In addition, the National Security Council was created. This 1947 act created many of the organizational entities and much of the overarching structure that we recognize today.

However, some durable problems persisted beyond 1947. For example, much of the service-centric organizational structure that had been in evidence during World War II remained unaltered. At one point during World War II, the wartime Joint Chiefs consisted of General Hap Arnold (Army Air Forces), General George Marshall (Chief of Staff of the Army), Admiral William Leahy (Chief of Staff to the Commander in Chief, i.e. Roosevelt), and Admiral Ernest King (Chief of Naval Operations). The chiefs met to discuss a British suggestion that steel be diverted from the construction of large surface combatants—battleships and heavy cruisers—and instead diverted to the construction of smaller ships, primarily convoy escorts and landing craft.

Three of the Joint Chiefs—Arnold, Marshall, and Leahy—agreed with the British recommendation. Leahy observed that it appeared "the vote is three to one." King, speaking as the chief of the Navy, replied that the Joint Chiefs did not have the authority to vote on any issue where the Navy was concerned. In effect, King was asserting that the Chief of Naval Operations had a veto when he believed the interests of the Navy were profoundly concerned. It is noteworthy that King was disagreeing with a fellow naval officer, Leahy, when he asserted this claim.

This aspect of the military's culture at the time was also captured in Fleet Admiral William F. Halsey's testimony to a Senate committee in 1945.

> I, for one, am unwilling to have the Chief of the Army Air Force pass on the question of whether the Navy should have funds for building and maintaining a balanced fleet. One might as well ask a committee composed of a Protestant, a Catholic, and a Jew to save our national souls by recommending a national church or creed.[2]

The 1947 National Security Act left this service-centric organizational culture largely untouched.

This service parochialism was a primary target of the Goldwater-Nichols Act of 1986. Prior to the 1980s, each individual service was in control of its procurement and was largely immune to influence from the other services. As organizational behavior would predict, this was the way the services preferred it, since it gave them maximum latitude over what they requested from Congress. Thanks to Goldwater-Nichols, the military has achieved a measure of centralization and jointness in its acquisition process, a significant change from the way procurement was conducted decades ago.

This act also substantially empowered the position of the Chairman of the Joint Chiefs of Staff (CJCS). Following the act, the CJCS became the primary military advisor to the president and was invited to NSC meetings at the president's discretion. He was expected to honestly represent the opinions of the service chiefs. Under the new law, the CJCS was directed to generate an array of strategic plans and assessments, allowing the chairman numerous avenues by which to influence a wide spectrum of the DoD's functions.

Recognizing the important scope of these changes, the first post-Goldwater-Nichols Chairman—Admiral William Crowe—proceeded cautiously. Even when granted new authority, Crowe recognized that he must nevertheless consider how best to acclimate the Department of Defense to a profound change. Crowe maintained a period of inclusiveness with the Joint Chiefs, continuing the practice of only moving forward when there was unanimity. When he determined the time was right to offer his own advice independently of the will of his fellow chiefs for the first time, one observer recalls that Crowe "sweated blood" over the decision. Gradually, the position of CJCS was empowered to the point where the CJCS's dominant role over the Joint Staff today is unquestioned.

The Defense Budget

The authors of the U.S. Constitution imagined a nation with no standing army. The Constitution states that the government is permitted to "provide and maintain" a navy, but only to "raise and support" an army. There are a number of reasons for this language, but two stand out. First, the military technology available to land forces at the time—muskets and cannon—made it possible to muster infantry units on short notice that possessed some measure of battlefield potency. A second reason, of course, was the recent history of the early nation, for which the notion of a standing army was associated with British occupation. Permanent military forces on land were associated with subjugation, and the Constitution's framers wanted to minimize the risk of the military emerging as an oppressive institution.

Even at the time the Constitution was written, however, there were reservations from some of the framers regarding the wisdom of this quasi-prohibition against standing armies. Alexander Hamilton wrote in December 1787 about how a reliance on militias was likely to prove insufficient for the nation's security.

> The steady operations of war against a regular and disciplined army can only be successfully conducted by a force of the same kind. Considerations of economy, not less than of stability and vigor, confirm this position. . . . War, like most other things, is a science to be acquired and perfected by diligence, by perseverance, by time, and by practice.[3]

The perceptiveness of Hamilton's words has only increased over time. Today, the political debate has shifted light-years in the other direction, largely due to changes in military technology and the need to deter adversaries. A large standing force and defense budgets in excess of half a trillion dollars are now the normal state of affairs for the United States.

The defense industry plays a powerful role in decisions relating to the size of the military budget, and to military procurement. Because the U.S. defense budget is so large—the requested DoD budget for 2018 was $639.1 billion—there are many defense dollars to compete for. To help assure that they are competitive for future contracts, defense firms spend heavily on lobbying and campaign contributions. In 2016, defense contractors spent a total in excess of $127 million lobbying Congress and the White House on issues relevant to their industry. This lobbying effort by the industry helps ensure that defense budgets stay high and the cycle perpetuates itself.

Ironically, Dwight Eisenhower—the highest-ranking former military officer to reside at the White House in recent times—grew to be deeply concerned about the future influence of the military industrial complex in American governance. He offered the following warning three days before he left office in 1960, with words that are relevant today:

> Until the latest of our world conflicts, the United States had no armaments industry. American makers of plowshares could, with time and as required, make swords as well. But now we can no longer risk emergency improvisation of national defense; we have been compelled to create a permanent armaments industry of vast proportions. Added to this, three and a half million men and women are directly engaged in the defense establishment. We annually spend on military security more than the net income of all United States corporations.
>
> This conjunction of an immense military establishment and a large arms industry is new in the American experience. The total influence—economic, political, even spiritual—is felt in every city, every State house, every office of the Federal government. We recognize the imperative need for this development. Yet we must not fail to comprehend its grave implications. Our toil, resources and livelihood are all involved; so is the very structure of our society.
>
> In the councils of government, we must guard against the acquisition of unwarranted influence, whether sought or unsought, by the military-industrial complex. The potential for the disastrous rise of misplaced power exists and will persist.[4]

Ronald Reagan had almost the opposite perspective on the military. For Reagan, the fact the Soviets spent proportionately more of their national budget on the military put the United States at a strategic disadvantage, one he was determined to rectify. In his autobiography, he wrote of his concern that the military was seen as an unappealing career because soldiers were so poorly compensated. Only 69% of enlistees in 1980 had received a high school diploma, the lowest rate on record for the nation at the time. He talked of married enlisted personnel being forced to supplement their incomes with food stamps, and of service members who were so ashamed of their vocation that they removed their uniforms whenever they left the confines of their base.

Reagan's focus was on expanding and improving the military's capabilities. He was ultimately responsible for the largest peacetime military buildup in U.S. history. Reagan's initial request was for a five-year plan (1981–85) that would swell the defense budget by 55%, an unheard-of peacetime increase. In a potent indication of his success in convincing Congress and the nation of the correctness of his course, Reagan was ultimately sent a bill that authorized a 51% increase in the defense budget—strikingly close to his original request.

America loves to spend money on its military, and this fact has a significant impact on our national security policy. The public has grown to expect that U.S. service personnel will have the best equipment at their disposal, and no other national security department has remotely as much leverage on Capitol Hill as the DoD. Before he left office, Secretary of Defense Robert Gates noted the imbalance that this mentality creates in American national security policy. He went so far as to recommend, in remarks offered before Congress, that Congress increase the budget of the State Department even if it was at the expense of the Department of Defense. While it is commonplace for cabinet secretaries to recommend that Congress spend more on the department they represent, it is extremely rare—Gates called his own statement "heresy"—for a sitting cabinet member to offer Congress such direct guidance on the overall distribution of the federal budget. Gates thought the funding imbalance deserved Congress's fullest attention.

Military Procurement

How does the Executive Branch influence the procurement process, the means by which the military arms itself? Creating a sense of urgency behind a particular weapons system is an avenue by which a president can seek to orient the public debate on a system, in hopes of generating pressure on Congress for approval. Reagan's endorsement and promotion of the "Star Wars" antiballistic missile system is an example. Reagan extolled the potential benefits of such a system, arguing in speeches that it was immoral to fail to use the United States' technical acumen to generate potential defenses against Armageddon.

In a 23 March 1983 speech, Reagan said, "I call upon the scientific community in our country, those who gave us nuclear weapons, to turn their great talents now to the cause of mankind and world peace." It was a proposal that was controversial to many, and derided as a technological fantasy by others. However, the president's call for a new defensive system ultimately could not be ignored, and Congress eventually appropriated funds for the program.

Merely proposing the system arguably had a strategic impact. Some historical studies of the Soviet Union suggest that Reagan's rhetoric altered the Soviets' perception of U.S. power, since the USSR consistently overestimated the likely effectiveness of the missile defense program. Anatoly Dobrynin, the former Soviet ambassador to the United States, believed that his country's leadership was convinced of the gravity of Reagan's decision, and claimed senior Soviet officials "treated Reagan's statement as a real threat."

Not all decisions regarding the size of the military are made in the structured environment of the budget process. At times, a sudden requirement for a cut in the defense budget can lead to a consequential decision being made outside of normal processes. For example, a senior DoD official once offered the following anecdote. He received a call from the Department of Defense Comptroller shortly after noon on an unremarkable workday (the Comptroller is the chief financial and budgetary advisor for the Secretary of Defense, and holds the rank of Undersecretary). The Comptroller told the former senior official that the president had been in a meeting that morning, and as a consequence of a budget deal the president had struck with some members of Congress, it would be necessary to pare $1.5 billion from the defense budget by the end of the day.

Obviously, this is a highly unusual method of adjusting the defense budget. A deadline of three or four hours does not permit the usual studies that might normally inform the shift of such a significant sum. In this case, rapid decisions were made—based on personal experience and deep familiarity with the options available—and a major weapons platform was set aside for early retirement by the end of the afternoon.

At times, presidents have the ability to resist even a full-court press by a coalition of military officers and influential Congressmen. During the Kennedy administration, senior Air Force officers were eager to build a fleet of 150 B-70 Valkyries, a plane that would deliver nuclear weapons to the Soviet Union at speeds of up to 2,000 miles an hour. General Curtis LeMay, then USAF Chief of Staff, was certain that the United States needed the plane, and he had a powerful ally in Rep. Carl Vinson, the Chairman of the House Armed Services Committee. It was a daunting political combination, but Kennedy was determined to have his way, in part because he had come to distrust LeMay's judgment. Kennedy also believed Congress was encroaching on his power as commander-in-chief by forcing him to procure the system in quantity.

On 19 March 1962, the day before a crucial vote on the B-70's fate, Kennedy invited Vinson to the White House. Greeting him as "Mr. Chairman," Kennedy asked if the congressman would be satisfied if a letter could be placed in the record stating Vinson's concerns. Vinson demurred, at which point Kennedy invited him for a private walk in the Rose Garden. No one knows what was said, but when the two men returned, Vinson was willing to change the proposed language in the legislation to an "authorization" to spend funds on the B-70, without directing the president to do so.

This example illustrates an important point about the division of power and authority between the Legislative and Executive Branches. The issue of who holds what authority is not self-enforcing, but instead requires the empowered party to contest an issue when one arises. Kennedy could have decided it was politically imprudent to confront Vinson over this issue, and the B-70 might then be recalled by historians as a precedent that weakened the president's role as commander-in-chief. Instead, it is a procurement contest lost to history, not even worthy of an index entry in most biographies of Kennedy.

Congress has a significant role to play in the president's control of the military—over the declaration of war, over the structure of the military, and over budgetary and spending decisions. This last area is one where Congress carefully guards its role. However, outside of these spheres, the president usually has potent advantages in debates over how to manage the military to serve the nation's security interests.

Notes

1 David R. Mayhew, *Divided We Govern: Party Control, Lawmaking, and Investigations, 1946–1990* (New Haven: Yale University Press, 1991), p. 112.
2 Peter J. Roman and David W. Tarr, "The Joint Chiefs of Staff: From Service Parochialism to Jointness," *Political Science Quarterly*, Vol. 113, no. 1 (1998), p. 93.
3 Alexander Hamilton, *Federalist No. 25*, 21 December 1787.
4 Dwight D. Eisenhower, "Farewell Address," 17 January 1961.

2

THE PEACETIME MILITARY

While the ultimate task of the Department of Defense is to prepare for war, day-to-day operations tend to find the department on a peacetime footing (one hopes). Managing the military during times of relative quiet affords certain advantages. National security priorities may be selected with due consideration, reorganization initiatives and policy changes can be thoroughly vetted, and a wide array of opinions can be gathered on any proposal. Past errors can be assessed, trends and developments analyzed, and decisions pondered in the absence of the heat of conflict. This chapter assesses the task of peacetime control of the military.

Steering a bureaucracy as massive as that of the Department of Defense is an onerous task. While wartime offers its own challenges to organizational change, peacetime does as well. Among these is the risk that relative calm can lull individuals and organizations into the mindset that dramatic change is unnecessary, and that the status quo is acceptable. That may well be the case. Bureaucracies are daunting things to change, and those most familiar with them know these challenges well. Consider the perspective of Donald Rumsfeld, as he took control of the Pentagon for the second time in his career during the George W. Bush administration:

> The topic today is an adversary that poses a threat, a serious threat, to the security of the United States of America. From a single capitol, it attempts to impose its demands across time zones, continents, oceans, and beyond. With brutal inconsistency, it stifles free thought,

and crushes new ideas. It disrupts the defense of the United States and places the lives of men and women in uniform at risk. . . . You may think I'm describing one of the last decrepit dictators of the world. But their day, too, is almost past, and they cannot match the strength and size of this adversary. The adversary's closer to home. It's the Pentagon bureaucracy.[1]

These remarks were delivered in the last quiet moment of his second term as secretary: 10 September 2001.

There are many ways to change organizations. One of the least durable, but sometimes the most effective, is to control who takes a position in the organization. Vice President Richard Cheney, having previously served in the White House as Chief of Staff and Secretary of Defense, understood the importance of mid- and lower-level officials in the Pentagon. Cheney biographer Barton Gellman recounts how the vice president sought out opportunities to place allies at less senior levels of the national security bureaucracy.

> In the policy fields that Cheney cared about, he found places for allies even deeper in the bureaucracy. He did it gently, by way of suggestions, not commands, to those who did the hiring. Most of the government's work, Cheney knew, never reached the altitude of Senate-confirmed appointees. Reliable people in midlevel posts would have the last word on numberless decisions about where to spend or not spend money, whom to regulate, how to enforce.[2]

An incoming presidential administration has a remarkable number of positions to fill. In parliamentary systems, a new government may need to find individuals for between 50 and 500 positions. In the U.S. Government, an incoming president can fill more than 5,000 positions with political appointees, should he or she choose to do so.

Though the president ostensibly controls all that happens in the Executive Branch—and is certainly politically liable for all Executive Branch actions—the individuals who staff the bureaucracy will have a large amount of input in a variety of ways, during peacetime or wartime. The executive branch staff will determine organizational procedures, decide which issues need to be resolved at a higher level, present policy options, and decide what information is reliable and important. They will hire, and sometimes fire, at lower levels. These are potentially potent decisions, possibly leading the government in directions the president did not intend. This is the irony of the presidency—total control is encumbered with staggering limitations on one's access to information, as well as on one's understanding of how the bureaucracy is actually functioning.

Presidents have taken different positions regarding sub-cabinet level appointments. During the George W. Bush presidency, partly influenced by Vice President Cheney's understanding of the Executive Branch, considerable attention was paid to sub-cabinet level appointments, as discussed above. Contrast this with the approach initially taken by the Nixon administration, where President Richard Nixon initially delegated staffing decisions to his cabinet secretaries. According to one account, Nixon immediately regretted this action.

> President Nixon, at an early cabinet meeting, announced that appointment authority would be vested in the cabinet. Immediately after making his announcement he turned to an aide and said: 'I just made a big mistake.' H.R. Haldeman [Nixon's Chief of Staff] wanted to control the appointments process more closely, but he was not able to stay on top of it. 'It just happened by inertia; we just had too much to do.'[3]

Personnel decisions outside of the Department of Defense can have a profound impact on defense matters as well. For example, the selection of Elbridge Durbrow and Frederick Nolting as ambassadors to South Vietnam from 1957 to 1963 may have had a significant impact on U.S. policy. Durbrow was initially an enthusiast of South Vietnamese President Ngo Dinh Diem, but his perception changed greatly once he had served some months in South Vietnam. Diem showed little aptitude for the nation-building that the South desperately required, and Durbrow explained this to Washington. Nolting, in contrast, stood behind Diem unconditionally—which had the effect of reducing pressure on Diem to engage in needed reforms. The Saigon government's subsequent lack of progress made Diem's fall from grace in Washington and subsequent removal from power more likely, which destabilized the south and paved the way for greater U.S. military engagement in the country. In effect, the president's choice of ambassador contributed to the probability of military escalation.

Though there are numerous areas where the military plays a role in peacetime foreign policy, the remainder of this chapter focuses on three: military signals sent during peacetime, organizational behavior, and long-term strategic planning. Counterterrorism actions will be dealt with in a later chapter.

Military Signaling

Both consciously and inadvertently, the military sends innumerable signals to a myriad array of audiences during peacetime. Decisions about what weapons to buy and where to deploy forces are signals that are quickly digested by adversaries and allies alike. The military is perhaps unique in its ability to signal U.S. policy, in that military decisions often involve moving physical elements of the United States' national security apparatus. While a decision to issue a demarche may or may not indicate a genuine policy commitment, a military redeployment involves a physical commitment, and one that can be observed. This is not to say that military maneuvers are never intended to deceive. Moreover, sometimes redeployments are ignored, or fail to communicate the intended signal. Nevertheless, maneuvering an Army brigade closer to harm's way can signal a policy commitment in a more significant way than a presidential statement.

Even beyond the signals that a military can send via specific actions, it is also possible to alter an enemy's strategic perception gradually over time—potentially in ways that are unintended (as well as destabilizing) for the broader relationship. These signals can raise the risk of crisis escalation, and presidents would be well served to remain vigilant against them. The Cold War offers a number of examples along this line (some of which are explored in later chapters), but one is of particular use for understanding the potential dangers of inadvertent military signals.

In 1990, the president's Foreign Intelligence Advisory Board (FIAB) finished a classified report titled "The Soviet 'War Scare.'"[4] It asserted that an array of developments in U.S. military capabilities (primarily in the nuclear realm) during Ronald Reagan's tenure in office had convinced many senior leaders in the Soviet Union that the United States sought to develop the capability to launch a successful surprise nuclear attack on the USSR. The Soviet mindset was compounded by President Ronald Reagan's unsparing rhetoric toward the USSR; Reagan had recently offered his iconic assertion that the Soviet Union was an "evil empire." These factors conspired to create a fearful and vulnerable mentality in the Soviet leadership, to the point where they feared that the United States was considering a sudden, decapitating strike. In nuclear parlance, the United States would be able to initiate a "splendid first strike"—a nuclear first strike that was so successful in eliminating the Soviet nuclear capability that the United States would suffer little or no damage in return.

It was in this strategic environment that the United States conducted a NATO exercise, titled Able Archer, in November 1983. Able Archer was designed to test new communications methods, and it involved live mobilization exercises of U.S. forces in Europe. All of this would have been observed by Soviet spies, who had been specifically ordered on 8 or 9 November to look for signs of a heightened NATO alert status in Europe and, in particular, to report indications of an impending nuclear attack. The declassified 1990

American review concluded that previous U.S. reports had underestimated the extent to which the Soviets had been deeply fearful of the possibility that the United States would seek to launch a surprise attack against the USSR. In terms of inadvertent military signals contributing to an unstable geostrategic environment, this is as bad as it gets. The foundation of nuclear deterrence between the superpowers rested on the expectation that one side was incapable of launching an attack that would eliminate the other side's ability to offer a devastating retaliation. Able Archer was intended to send a signal of NATO's readiness to defend Western Europe. However, because Moscow was deeply concerned about American intentions, the military exercise sent a signal the senders did not intend to convey. The stakes were high—had the situation escalated, a catastrophic conflict could have resulted. This Cold War example offers an illustration of how an administration must be ever cognizant of how military actions can send unintended signals that potentially increase the risk of conflict.

Organizational Behavior: A Boon and a Trap

The military is an organization. As such, it exhibits aspects of organizational behavior—behavior that makes possible the complex and dangerous operations that are inherent in military action. However, this necessary element of organizational behavior can also obstruct and inhibit the execution of other missions that the president may deem in the national interest. Despite the seriousness inherent in the task of national security, the military is not immune to the proclivities of organizational behavior.

Consider an assessment made by Admiral George W. Anderson, who rose to the office of Chief of Naval Operations. Anderson was in that post during some of the most tense days of the Cold War—the Cuban Missile Crisis of October 1962. Despite having a position of great responsibility and influence during that crucial time, he more fondly recalled his time as commander of the Sixth Fleet in the Mediterranean from 1959–61. It was this posting, he said in hindsight, that was the "[m]ost interesting and even the *most important* assignment I had throughout my naval career . . . more interesting than being Chief of Naval Operations."[5] Anderson offers a fascinating perspective that must have been profoundly influenced by a long career immersed in the Navy's culture: he believed leading a fleet was more *important* than having a more senior position during one of the momentous junctures of history, and claimed that the subordinate position of fleet commander was even "more interesting."

Some clichés about the military should be dispensed with. It is not true that senior military leaders are always yearning for a fight, seeing action as the solution to every problem. Often, the opposite is true: senior officers are wary of civilian leaders who may underestimate the risks of action, and who may too casually view the military as a tool to be readily applied to the world's problems. While she was Secretary of State, Madeleine Albright complained that Chairman of the Joint Chiefs General Colin Powell had a habit of making military interventions in the Balkans seem too risky or too expensive. She later addressed a famous exchange she had had with the general:

> When we asked what it would take to free Sarajevo airport from the surrounding Serb artillery, he replied consistent with his commitment to the doctrine of overwhelming force, saying it would take tens of thousands of troops, cost billions of dollars, probably result in numerous casualties, and require a long and open-ended commitment of U.S. forces. Time and again he led us up the hill of possibilities and dropped us off on the other side with the practical equivalent of 'No can do.' After hearing this for the umpteenth time, I asked in exasperation, 'What are you saving this superb military for, Colin, if we can't use it?' Powell wrote in his memoirs that my question nearly gave him an "aneurism" and that he had to explain "patiently" to me the role of America's military.[6]

Albright's frustration may have been well-founded. At the same time, it is perfectly possible that Powell was always right, even on the umpteenth occasion.

An overview of some relevant organizational behavioral concepts can help shed light on how organizational behavior can impact a president's ability to effectively control the military. Organizations have interests, and the military is certainly no exception in this regard. Organizations identify their primary missions within the larger rubric of government activities, and seek to maximize their ability to perform that identified mission set. Anything that can aid the organization's ability to execute (or prepare to execute) its given task will be something the organization will seek to acquire or to assimilate. In contrast, anything that threatens the organization's ability to perform that mission—a competing organization, a threatened budget cut, a hostile civilian leader, or the like—will be something that the organization will seek to confront or counteract.

Organizations will also usually seek to avoid tasks that could dilute their core mission, or that may syphon a portion of their budget toward a weapon system that impinges on their ability to perform the organization's core function. Sometimes, this can lead to procurement positions that are strikingly counter-intuitive. For example, in the early 1960s, President Kennedy sought to accelerate the production of Polaris submarines from three per year to ten per year. Navy officers, without impugning the wisdom of the accelerated production, asserted that Polaris was no longer a Navy program, but a national program. These naval officers' position was pure organizational behavior—the submarines would be built in any event, given that Polaris was a presidential priority. In that case, why not have Polaris funded as a national system, thereby preserving the Navy's budget for traditional Navy priorities? The fact that Polaris was being promoted by a president who had served in the Navy during World War II made no difference.

Organizational behavior often dictates what military officers see as their most pressing duty when they are engaged in budgetary or procurement disputes with what Washington calls "the interagency." The interagency refers to any cooperative effort between two or more departments or agencies within the executive branch. For example, the reconstruction of Iraq was an interagency effort, since it combined the skills and efforts of the Departments of State, Defense, Treasury, and others. Military officers assigned to interagency jobs—that is, positions that involve negotiations with other departments in order to collectively achieve a desired outcome—tend to assume that their default position should be to protect the position and budget equities of the military organization they represent. This point is true not just for military staffs, but civilian organizations as well. As one military officer once put it to me: "The easiest way to get on your boss's bad side is to fail to defend your organization's equity. So you play it safe and boring all the time." If the military's budget is unharmed at the end of the day, that can be considered a win, even if a pressing national security priority fell by the wayside.

This aspect of organizational behavior can have a profound influence on the military as an organization. Keep in mind that military officers join the service to defend the nation on the battlefield. Protecting the broader national interest in an interagency dispute—which could, in some instances, involve sacrificing a position long held by an agency in order to serve the nation's greater good—is often not a priority. Even if an officer can identify a greater national good, there are often few career incentives to work toward that end. A bad military fitness report could easily follow, and damage to one's career is something that individuals in any vocation are unlikely to casually embrace. As a result, officers face significant incentives to represent their specific agency's interest—even when this means the outcome is contrary to the national interest.

Even when the strategic environment evolves to allow for a reconsideration of weapons stockpiles, budget sizes, and the like, conservatism and risk-avoidance can lead officers to see these opportunities as unappealing. A budget share lost is very hard to regain. Budget cuts are a threat, often one that is of more concern to the organization in question that any geostrategic opponent. Legend has it that in 1964 Air Force General Curtis LeMay asked an aide, "Tell me, son, who is our enemy?" "The Soviet Union, sir," the aide replied. LeMay smiled sadly and shook his head. "No, son, the Soviets are our adversary. Our enemy is the Navy."

Advances in technology are considered not just for the military opportunity they offer, but also for their potential impact on a service's share of the budget. Consider the following assessment of budget debates between the Air Force and the Navy in the late 1940s.

> The Air Force was lobbying for defense resources to be devoted to airpower, while the Navy and Army were anxious lest over-reliance on atom bombs resulted in the neglect of provisions for traditional forms of warfare. . . . The new Air Force recognized the bomb to be their strongest bargaining card and played it for all it was worth, carefully fudging the question of whether the vast destructive power concentrated in a single device ought really to allow for contraction, rather than expansion, in numbers of aircraft. The other services felt this competition keenly in the tough struggle to keep forces intact and prepare for the future in the atmosphere of post-war demobilization and budgetary stringency. The Navy was particularly anxious to secure support for its own expensive investment program, for 'super-carriers,' and felt it had little choice but to oppose the Air Force and its atomic strategy head-on. . . . The Navy was seen as parochial and backward-looking, desperate to justify its existence in a world in which the reach of airpower was being extended all the time, and in which the most likely enemy was virtually land-locked and had only a slight maritime tradition.[7]

Atomic weapons were viewed as opportunities or threats—not to the nation's security, but to each service's share of the defense budget.

Presidents must be alert to the myriad ways that organizational behavior can affect the military, including the president's control of the military. It should be reiterated that organizational behavior, properly managed, is essential to any group performing a complex and dangerous task. War is, without doubt, one such task. Nevertheless, any civilian leader of the military must be aware of the potential pitfalls of organizational behavior. The time when organizational behavior's proclivities can be most safely countered is often during peacetime, before leaders decide to let slip the dogs of war.

The Challenge of Long-Term Strategy

It is a common presidential ambition to find a grand strategy for their administration, one that clearly lays out significant but achievable goals and the means to achieve them. The idea that national security policy can be rationally governed by a road map is a comforting one, for it suggests that the ship of state can be navigated by a steady hand at the wheel. In reality, even a finely-crafted set of strategic ends and means must be revised in the face of a dynamic strategic environment. This is, arguably, a bias in U.S. political culture—the expectation that presidents can set long-term plans in motion that will address the globe's problems and make the world a better place.

One of the documents that is most commonly cited as representing a presidential road map for national security policy is the National Security Strategy (NSS). President Bill Clinton was a prolific author of strategic ideas, and his administration generated a new NSS approximately every year. Successive presidents have tended to prefer issuing one NSS per term in office. Despite its prominence, the document's strategic utility is sharply limited, however. It is highly public and must take into consideration all potential interpretations by all audiences, both foreign and domestic. In a swiftly evolving strategic environment, even well-crafted documents can be overtaken by events.

2001 offered a telling example of how the NSS can quickly be rendered irrelevant. If 9/11 had been delayed by several months, a freshly-minted Bush National Security Strategy would have been published—and, following al Qaeda's attack, promptly consigned to the recycling bin. The actions of nineteen individual attackers on that terrible day amply illustrate the vulnerability of strategic plans. While the Bush administration was not utterly dismissive of the terrorist threat prior to 9/11, there are many who argue that Bush's senior officials viewed terrorism as an overstated problem, and turned their focus to other national security threats.

As we now know, 9/11 also altered policymakers' perceptions of the threat posed by countries that had nothing to do with the attacks. According to Todd Purdum, notes taken by Rumsfeld's aides during a meeting on 9/11 show a defense secretary considering a global response, one that included confronting Iraq.

> Best Info fast. Judge whether good enough to hit S.H. [Saddam Hussein] at same time . . . not only OBL [Osama bin Laden]. Go massive. Sweep it all up. Things related and not.

Similarly, in Douglas Feith's memoir *War and Decision*, Feith (an Undersecretary of Defense at the time) cites his notes of a meeting on the weekend of

15 September 2001, where senior administration officials talked of creating a "shockwave" and a "sustained, broad campaign" that would "surprise people."

These examples illustrate how dramatic events can rapidly alter the strategic perceptions of even experienced policymakers, sometimes in areas unrelated to the event itself. The strategic priorities that these individuals had ruminated on for years—China, Russia—were quickly supplanted. In effect, their peacetime assessments of the proper focus of U.S. national security policy were upended by events—an attack that was carried out not by a rival nation, but by a small group of individuals armed with box cutters.

This points to the most sobering lesson an incoming president could learn from the United States' involvement in Iraq. At times, one's duty as president is to resist those who speak insistently of threats that must be confronted. The military can be an alluring tool for American presidents; it can be tempting to sweep aside nettlesome problems with military force. In his memoir, President Bush relates a conversation he had with Vice President Cheney shortly before the invasion of Iraq. Cheney, frustrated with the pace of diplomacy and with Saddam Hussein's seeming intransigence on the issue of weapons of mass destruction, asked Bush "Are you going to take care of this guy, or not?" In the end, the mirage of a quick military solution to an exaggerated threat was too tempting, and America's vast military apparatus was sent into action to "take care of this guy."

Even a carefully considered peacetime strategic shift, such as President Obama's "pivot to Asia," can go awry. The intent of the shift had a rational purpose—to focus more strategic energy and resources on what was seen as a region of growing importance, Asia. The pivot's secondary (and less trumpeted) goal was to de-emphasize the role of the Middle East in America's grand strategy. Yet there were unforeseen consequences of the pivot. Asian nations, instead of genuflecting to the additional American "gravity" that Obama sought to impart on U.S. policy in the region, became fearful of the United States' intentions. According to many observers, China has reacted to Washington's shifting of 60% of U.S. naval and air assets to the region as a threatening development that must be confronted. Middle Eastern states, especially America's closer allies, became alarmed at the prospect of the United States' potential disengagement with the region.

With these examples in mind, one might consider the following maxims as they relate to the purported utility of strategic documents.

1. The broader the intended audience of the document, the more watered-down and unhelpful it is likely to be. Such documents are vetted by a wide array of departments and agencies. Wide government vetting often

renders the document as politically safe as possible, potentially neutering it in the process.

2. The less frequently the strategy is updated, the less useful it will be. Genuinely useful strategic assessments are rarely produced on a schedule mandated by U.S. law.

3. A bold or innovative strategic idea is unlikely to be revealed in such public documents. Agencies will promote their ideas behind the scenes, and not introduce them in a National Security Strategy.

4. Strategic documents almost never argue, "It is wisest to do nothing in the face of this threat." This is true even when "doing nothing" is both a wise recommendation and an accurate summation of U.S. policy to date. There can be a significant bias toward extolling the benefits of proactive foreign policy, perhaps nowhere more evident than in the nation's broad-gauge strategic documents. It is worth keeping in mind that the most significant example of a post-9/11 proactive policy choice was the invasion of Iraq in 2003.

Regarding this last point, consider how the U.S. military assesses the threat posed by China. It is not the military's task to explore how China might become a reliable partner to the U.S., or how it might be possible to overstate the threat posed by China. In terms of threat assessment, the military is in the business of looking for worst-case scenarios, both in the short term and the long term, and everywhere in between. The important task of developing weapons systems—especially systems that might be deployed against a large and sophisticated military like the People's Liberation Army—demands both time and money. As a nation, we have developed a national security culture that holds that it is prudent and necessary to stay ahead of military competitors and potential enemies.

For a wealthy and powerful nation, one that can afford to be vigilant against threats that may not require vigilance, this could be the best route—an expensive route, but a safe one. The risk this approach embraces is the possibility that an unnecessary confrontation is made more likely by a strategic culture that considers tolerable threats to be intolerable. America's defeat in Vietnam should have taught us that dominoes do not necessarily fall, and that worst-case scenarios do not always come to pass. America's debacle in Iraq should have taught us about our own ability to overstate threats. However, these lessons are not to be found in long-term strategy documents. National Security Strategies are devoted instead to current fears and concerns, some well-founded and some less so. Presidents and citizens alike would do well to accept these documents with that caveat in mind.

Notes

1 Matthew Moten, *Presidents and Their Generals: An American History of Command in War* (Cambridge, MA: Harvard University Press, 2014), p. 349.
2 Barton Gellman, *Angler: The Cheney Vice Presidency* (New York: Penguin Press, 2008), p. 39.
3 James P. Pfiffner, *The Strategic Presidency: Hitting the Ground Running* (Lawrence, KS: University Press of Kansas, 1996), p. 67.
4 The report has since been declassified.
5 George W. Anderson, "Copy of Oral History," *Oral History, Naval Historical Collection, Naval War College,* Vol. 2, no. 42A, p. 377. Typescript published 1980. Emphasis added.
6 Madeleine Albright, *Madam Secretary* (New York: Miramax Books, 2003), pp. 181–2.
7 Lawrence Freedman, *The Evolution of Nuclear Strategy* (New York: St. Martin's Press, 1981), p. 29.

3

COUNTERTERRORISM AND DRONE WARFARE

Secret operations during what would otherwise be called peacetime have been a tool of the American presidency since the inception of the nation. George Washington, the nation's first president, had been his own spymaster during the Revolutionary War. Once he became president, he requested (and received) a secret "Contingency Fund" for use in whatever covert activities the president deemed necessary. The fund was initially $40,000, a healthy sum at the nation's founding. This fund permitted President Washington to hire secret agents, buy intelligence, and undertake other activities that Washington deemed should best not become public (or Congressional) knowledge.

The post-9/11 security environment creates clear incentives for the employment of limited force in counterterrorism operations. The breadth of interpretation presidents have accorded Congress's post-9/11 authorization of the use of military force allows the president to employ the military against any entity with even the most tenuous connection to al Qaeda. At the same time, irregular counterterrorism operations can create unintentional political and strategic commitments. This can be politically awkward at the least and strategically perilous at worst. The purpose of engaging in a covert operation is usually to avoid having the action in question attributed to the nation that perpetrates it. Nevertheless, covert action can obtain a policy inertia of sorts, luring one to make further commitments that may have seemed less appealing at the outset of the operation.

On the afternoon of 9/11, as the United States reeled from a devastating and shocking attack, defense officials conducted a hasty news conference in the Pentagon to reassure the wounded nation. Among those who spoke was

Chairman of the Joint Chiefs of Staff General Hugh Shelton. When his turn came, he stated "I will tell you up front, I have no intentions of discussing today what comes next . . . but make no mistake about it: your armed forces are ready." In important respects, Shelton was right. This was a moment when decades of investment in readiness, in distant strike capability, and in a host of other areas would come into play.

The head of Central Command on 9/11, General Tommy Franks, titled the first post-9/11 chapter of his memoir "A New Kind of War." Franks noted the inaccessibility of the landlocked country of Afghanistan, and the fact that Afghanistan's tall mountains made helicopter operations very difficult. Nevertheless, the United States would not be without advantages:

> As my staff and I reviewed our options in September 2001, I could not think of a historical parallel for the military campaign under consideration. The operation represented a revolution in warfighting. We would introduce the most advanced military technology in the world . . . onto one of the world's most primitive battlefields.[1]

Franks' statement perhaps epitomizes one of the significant pressures facing a president wielding American military might in the struggle against terrorism. If preventing another major terrorist attack on the U.S. continues to be a major national security goal—and there is every reason to think this will be the case—then confronting terrorist organizations in distant lands, where threats can be stopped at their earlier stages, will be a major element of American counterterrorism strategy.

The focus on counterterrorism has greatly increased the role and level of activity of Special Operations Command (SOCOM). In the years since 9/11, significant investments have been made in special operations forces (SOF), the major element in the U.S. military that handles many of the operations that have come to define the struggle against terrorism. Special Operations are defined by SOCOM as "the use of small units in direct or indirect military actions that are focused on strategic or operational objectives." SOCOM draws forces from the Army, Air Force, Navy, and the Marines. When they were introduced, the services had often been dismissive of the potential role of SOF, believing they were a distraction from the need to prepare for a major confrontation with Soviet land forces during the Cold War. However, in the late 1980s, Senators Sam Nunn and William Cohen, with Representative Dan Daniel, became active proponents of SOF's importance. President Ronald Reagan subsequently established a new independent combatant command, and SOCOM was activated in June 1987.

Since 9/11, SOF have completed a remarkable transition: from the military's unwanted stepchild after World War II, to the element of the military that has seen the largest percentage increase in assigned service personnel since 9/11. By 2012, SOCOM had been assigned double the pre-9/11 number of troops. During the same period, SOCOM's budget increased from $3.5 billion in 2001 to $10.5 billion. SOCOM and related SOF units have been remarkably active, having operated in over seventy-five countries since 9/11. SOCOM's level of deployment is one of the elements of President Barack Obama's military posture that President Donald Trump has left practically unaltered.

The appeal of using SOF for countering terrorist threats is clear. The use of SOF allows for quiet insertion and small logistical footprints, as well as the potential for a brisk exit. Given that terrorist organizations are often located in countries where the national government has imperfect control over its territory—such as Syria, Yemen, and Somalia—the international backlash from SOF raids can be expected to be modest and tolerable.

This is the new territory that the United States finds itself in, simultaneously comfortable and awkward. Comfortable in the sense that we consider ourselves policing where no one else can, and violating international norms where no one of consequence will complain. However, it is awkward territory as well: the United States has chosen to engage in a regular pace of military actions in foreign countries, blurring the line between war and peace. The frequency of these actions can be striking. In June 2010, General David Petraeus, then commander of coalition forces in Afghanistan, estimated that U.S.-led forces were launching approximately one "kinetic action" per day against targets in the country. Yet these actions are often ignored, since only a tiny fraction of those attacks made the evening news.

Many of the military actions conducted by SOF have been justified under the authorization for the use of force passed by Congress on 14 September 2001, which offered wide latitude to the government to pursue any and all individuals even remotely connected with the 9/11 attacks. The American public has shown little concern over the scope of government activities that have been justified by this act. President Obama used it over a decade after 9/11 to justify employing the military against ISIS in Iraq and Syria, even though ISIS, as an organization, did not exist on 11 September 2001. It seems clear that irregular actions will continue to be the regular business of the United States military.

While this may be necessary in many instances, there are potential repercussions. The casual violation of international norms, such as sovereignty and the significance of borders, can lead to new norms being established. The

American penchant for feeling free to pursue terrorist organizations into other states has not gone unnoticed. Military actions, even defensible ones, can set a precedent which could be utilized in ways that run counter to American interests.

The post-9/11 struggle against terrorism has led to increased reliance on a weapon system that combines surveillance and strike capability with political convenience: Unmanned Aerial Vehicles (UAVs), or drones. It is a solution to the problem of how to accurately target terrorists in remote areas, while attempting to minimize the risk of civilian casualties. It is also a way to avoid the dangers of aerial patrols and the limitations of piloted aircraft. To adapt a phrase Eliot Cohen used in 1994 when describing America's affection for air power, drones offer "gratification without commitment." As vast sums of money are invested in counterterrorism equipment, it was almost a foregone conclusion that a high-tech and mass-produced solution would be found.

To be sure, there are legal and normative pitfalls that face this new technology. In a (probably belated) attempt to avoid some of these negative connotations, the U.S. Air Force adopted the term "Remotely Piloted Vehicle," or RPV, in an effort to emphasize that there is pilot involved in the weapon system and to de-emphasize the mechanistic connotations of the technology. Perhaps the most inestimable repercussion of drone strikes is the potential for such attacks to cause resentment and anger that then inspires individual terrorists, motivates terrorist organizations, and contributes to the likelihood of future attacks. The impact is potentially broad. Retired General Stanley McChrystal, the former American commander in Afghanistan, has claimed that drone strikes "are hated on a visceral level, even by people who've never seen one or seen the effects of one." In nations such as Pakistan, the nation-wide media coverage of the drone campaign is roundly critical, as one might expect. One study suggests that access to media coverage is a stronger determinant of whether a Pakistani citizen is likely to oppose the American drone campaign than are the individual's religious sentiments. Protests against U.S. drone strikes often feature signs in English, suggesting an effort by the protesters to influence the international community. This points to a profound challenge for any president disposed to support these irregular actions: the benefits of a strike may seem immediate and easily achieved, but the long-term consequences are difficult to estimate and potentially profound.

Successful efforts to capture suspected terrorists, instead of launching military strikes, have been successful at times. In June 2014, U.S. Special Operations forces captured Ahmed Abu Khattala, the man believed to have been the key planner behind the attack on an American consulate in Benghazi, Libya in 2012. Capturing suspects in foreign countries is time-consuming and risky, but successful apprehensions are less likely to violate international norms and lead to unfavorable publicity. Yet the appeal of UAVs as a key component in America's global counterterrorism strategy means that they are likely to remain on the front lines. The remainder of this chapter addresses this rapidly growing element in the United States' counterterrorism arsenal.

Drones: America's Newest Weapon of Choice

How should we think of the military use of drones? Many see drones as epitomizing the militarization of America's foreign policy. They are viewed by some as soulless machines, allowing the United States to kill at will. Though America's drone campaign—a campaign significantly escalated under President Obama's leadership—has led to numerous civilian casualties, this in and of itself is not a reason to view the weapons as particularly immoral. If the alternative to a drone strike is a raid, or an invasion followed by occupation, those approaches often lead to civilian casualties as well.

The British Bureau of Investigative Journalism (BIJ) examined what it believed were all 383 known drone strikes in Pakistan from 2004–12. Of the between 2,296 and 3,718 people who were killed in these attacks, the BIJ further estimated that between 416 and 960 civilians were among the dead. One must not casually reduce issues of morality to a ratio: each of those hundreds of deaths represents the mangled body of an individual the United States did not intend to kill.

However, as a weapon of war, how should we see these data? The International Committee of the Red Cross has estimated that ten civilians died for every combatant killed in all the conflicts of the twentieth century. Yet that list of conflicts is a broad dataset, one that includes purposefully immoral combatants such as Nazi Germany. A better comparison might be an assessment of civilian deaths from coalition strikes from manned aircraft in Afghanistan after 9/11. This estimation, published in the *Small Wars Journal*, put the ratio at fifteen civilian deaths for every combatant killed. A United Nations study painted a very different picture, claiming there was only one civilian casualty for every ten manned airstrikes. The lack of a clear comparison to drone combat in Afghanistan makes it a difficult task to set one's moral compass.

The pilots themselves offer an unexpected facet to the debate. Warplane pilots will speak of the inhuman nature of their brand of combat: they drop a bomb, relying on targeting information provided by others, and may never see what they have destroyed. RPV pilots, in contrast, make a study of the individuals they target, observing them and their behavior for hours, days, or even weeks. "I can look at their faces," said one, "[I] see these guys playing with their kids and wives." They view the aftermath, as bodies are recovered and mourned. In this dimension, at least, what appears to be an inhuman mode of warfare can be strikingly human, even intimate. I have spoken to drone operators who told of being haunted by UAV-launched missile strikes that only wound their intended targets, and of then watching gravely injured individuals attempt to drag themselves toward safety.

Decisions in this area of national security are essentially decisions regarding assassination. These are potentially uncomfortable decisions for a democratic nation that has a tradition of the rule of law. As with most legal issues, the definition of what is or is not considered acceptable is often subject to manipulation—particularly when the kill chain does not include a clear advocate for the targeted individual. Consider the following quote from Attorney general Eric Holder, who offered a justification for the targeting of Anwar al-Awlaki, an American cleric who was eventually tracked to Yemen. Holder offers his interpretation of the term "imminent threat," a term that is used to justify rapid military action.

> The evaluation of whether an individual presents an 'imminent threat' incorporates considerations of the relevant window of opportunity to act, the possible harm that missing the window would cause civilians, and the likelihood of heading off future disastrous attacks against the United States.[2]

Holder, in a *post-hoc* attempt to justify drone attacks, turns the notion of imminence on its head. It is not the threat the potential target poses, but the imminent threat to the *opportunity* to attack the target. By this definition, a fleeting opportunity to attack a target who planned to conduct a terrorist operation years in the future could qualify as an imminent threat.

There are potential cognitive biases that a president should be aware of when making decisions in this area. It is easy to frame these decisions in ways that make them appear to be of pressing urgency, thereby removing the need for choice about whether or not to apply the military. Sometimes, the proposed target is a self-declared enemy of the United States, one who may have long espoused conflict and killing. Who knows what he will do in the future, whom he will inspire, how many Americans he will kill? An opportunity to strike is offered that poses little risk of collateral damage, perhaps an opportunity that will never present itself again. Phrasing the situation in these terms lightens the moral burden on the policymaker, since the decision practically makes itself.

President Obama, for at least a portion of his time in office, kept a "kill list" of individuals that he himself had personally authorized for the U.S. military (or other government agencies) to strike if the opportunity presented itself. According to a *New York Times* report, Obama had two motivations behind his decision to vet the list personally. First, before ordering a military strike to kill an individual, Obama felt an obligation to place the onus squarely on himself. Second, and perhaps no less important, he recognized that raising the "kill list" to the level of a presidential decision would have an impact on the level of attention the target selection process would receive from the federal bureaucracy. When those serving a president know their work will be personally weighed by the president, a higher standard of engagement and scrutiny is assured.

By at least one account, decisions about whether to authorize a military strike were first vetted outside of the president's purview, in video conference calls among numerous agency representatives. According to one participant, this was a highly unusual approach to a national security decision. Questions of how to define an individual's relationship to terrorism, and conflicts between agencies about who should be made a priority target, were common.

> It is the strangest of bureaucratic rituals: Every week or so, more than 100 members of the government's sprawling national security apparatus gather, by secure video conference, to pore over terrorist suspects' biographies and recommend to the president who should be the next to die.
>
> 'What's a Qaeda facilitator?' asked one participant, illustrating the spirit of the exchanges. 'If I open a gate and you drive through it, am I a facilitator?' Given the contentious discussions, it can take five or six sessions for a name to be approved, and names go off the list if a suspect no longer appears to pose an imminent threat, the official said. . . . The nominations go to the White House, where by [Obama's] own insistence and guided by Mr. Brennan, Mr. Obama must approve any name. . . . [Obama] believes that he should take moral responsibility for such actions. And he knows that bad strikes can tarnish America's image and derail diplomacy.[3]

The potential for a "bad strike" loomed large in the policy process. Errant strikes that kill innocents are exactly the sorts of actions that promote anti-American views. It should be noted that even strikes that generate no collateral damage can still scar the communities in which they take place, promoting the image of an all-pervasive American killing machine that cares nothing for the lives of non-Americans.

Some of the most senior officials involved in the process of deciding when drone strikes should be used have raised concerns that there is a temptation to abuse UAV strikes. When he was Director of National Intelligence, former Admiral Dennis Blair criticized some of those whom he believed were too eager to employ the military against distant and vulnerable targets. He felt the weapon was being promoted too casually as "the only game in town." To Blair, the United States' heavy reliance on drone strikes during the Obama administration reminded him uncomfortably of the military's use of body counts during the Vietnam War as an indicator of success.

Anwar al-Awlaki

Perhaps the most prominent drone strike was the attack that killed an American in Yemen: Anwar al-Awlaki. After 9/11, Awlaki's political perspective underwent a striking transition. Initially, Awlaki was seen as an American imam who could offer a moderate Muslim's perspective on issues for television reports. As an indicator of how moderate his views were at that time, he was invited to the Pentagon in February 2002 to speak about Islam. However, beginning in 2002, his views become more radical, and this contributed to his decision to leave the United States for the United Kingdom that year. He then moved from the UK to Yemen in approximately 2004, and his anti-American sermons gained a wide audience. Some linked Awlaki to Nidal Hasan, the man responsible for killing thirteen U.S. service members at Fort Hood in 2009. Awlaki was accused of serving as an inspiration and interlocutor for those that would attempt acts of violence.

Awlaki was added to the list of those targeted for killing in February 2010. At that time, Awlaki was the first and only American to be targeted by the military's post-9/11 drone campaign. It should be noted that the war against terrorism does not represent the first time that the United States has ordered military action in foreign countries knowing that U.S. citizens would be killed. During World War II, the U.S. military was fully aware that there were U.S. citizens serving with the German Army. This expectation did not change any targeting procedure or campaign plan. What is different in the post-9/11 drone campaign is the fact that individual American citizens are being selected and targeted, absent any legal proceeding.

Members of the Obama administration, and Obama himself, became convinced that Awlaki posed a unique threat to U.S. security.

What worried President Obama most was Awlaki's ingenuity in developing murderous schemes that could evade America's best defenses. Already he [Awlaki] had launched the Christmas Day plot. . . . Then, in October 2010, AQAP had managed to put improvised bombs—ink toner cartridges filled with explosive material—on cargo planes headed to the United States.

The standing orders [at that point] from Obama had always been to avoid collateral damage at almost any cost. . . . [But] Obama let it be known that he didn't want his options preemptively foreclosed. If there was a clear shot at the terrorist leader [Awlaki], even one that risked civilian deaths, he wanted to be advised of it. 'Bring it to me and let me decide in the reality of the moment rather than in the abstract,' he said, according to one confidant.[4]

This points to a core tension in the use of drones that encumbers presidential decisions regarding their use. The political and even strategic damage that an errant strike could cause is a significant concern. Yet it is difficult to set strict rules for the military in advance. In addition, even presidents who seek to avoid military conflict are leery of being seen as having missed an opportunity to take out a perceived threat. In America's national security culture, embracing the risk of ignoring a strike opportunity takes a unique brand of courage. Perhaps presidents will have to learn to find this courage, if the United States military is ever to seriously consider putting a halt to the current pace of counterterrorism drone strikes.

A U.S. drone killed Awlaki on 30 September 2011. From the standpoint of an incoming president considering future drone strikes, a critical question is: what was the net result of Awlaki's killing? A 2015 *New York Times* article suggested that Awlaki's influence was at least as strong as it had been before he was alive, and arguably his anti-American ideas had achieved even greater authority since his death. Many Islamic websites promptly pronounced him a martyr. In 2014, a nineteen-year-old man from Colorado was arrested while attempting to fly to Syria to join ISIS; it was later discovered he had left behind a number of DVDs of Awlaki's sermons. It is possible that Awlaki's killing led to an increase, and not a decrease, in his influence.

The weapon's availability, comparatively low cost, and limited direct risk to U.S. forces will make UAVs a tempting tool for many administrations to come. The American electorate seems largely inured to the moral concerns, and to the repercussions on America's reputation overseas. It is, of course, a president's job to take these considerations more seriously than the average voter.

When considering the elimination of terrorists or terrorist leaders, there is room to expect a tendency to overestimate the threat these individuals pose, and to underestimate the possibility that someone worse will follow. In the words of Warner Schilling and Jonathan Schilling, "In the end, decisions made in favor of assassination tend to be based on the hope, often without much evidence, that no successor to the assassinated figure could be worse and that any successor might be better."

As one might expect, America's drone campaign is widely unpopular beyond Pakistan as well. A Pew study from 2014 found that of forty-four countries surveyed, populations in thirty-nine of those nations disapproved of the United States' use of the technology. At the same time, the campaign has had less of an impact on America's image than one might expect. Of those same nations surveyed, 65% had a favorable view of the United States. Public opinion polls are never the sole determinants of whether or not to employ a tactic or weapon system, but they can foreshadow the long-term costs of today's actions.

Given the uneven nature of the threat posed by terrorist organizations, it is unsurprising that new weapons are being applied to the threat. Drones, in particular, offer unique advantages in the areas of surveillance and endurance. It is easy for the United States to continue on the current path, since the U.S. has a considerable technological lead. Future presidents should consider the rate at which the technological gap is closing, however. One estimate claimed that forty-one states had acquired drone systems in 2005. By 2012, the number had grown to seventy-six. There is room to speculate that the countries that will acquire the technology in the coming years are different from the early adaptors, who are more likely to be the more responsible—or at least the more deterrable—actors in the international arena.

In 1961, President John F. Kennedy responded to a recommendation that he authorize an effort to assassinate Cuban President Fidel Castro by saying "we can't get into that kind of thing, or we would all be targets." Given the rapid spread of drone technology, one must wonder if American policymakers will come to regret that a similar logic did not inform the United States' use of what may be a transitory advantage in drone technology.

Notes

1 Tommy Franks with Malcolm McConnell, *American Soldier* (New York: Harper-Collins, 2004), p. 262.
2 Attorney General Eric Holder, "Speech as Northwestern School of Law," 5 March 2012. Though the speech postdates the attack that killed Awlaki, it reflected an interpretation of imminence that was specifically developed to target Awlaki.
3 Jo Becker and Scott Shane, "Secret 'Kill List' Proves a Test of Obama's Principles and Will," *New York Times*, 29 May 2012.
4 Daniel Klaidman, "Drones: The Silent Killers," *Newsweek*, 28 May 2012.

4

THE CRUCIBLE OF CRISIS

On 10 October 1994, a delegation sent by President Bill Clinton—consisting of former President Jimmy Carter, former Senator Sam Nunn, and former Chairman of the Joint Chiefs Colin Powell—met with General Raoul Cedras, leader of the Haitian military junta that had prevented elected President Jean-Bertrand Aristide from returning to power. Clinton had become increasingly frustrated with the Haitian military's defiance of democratic norms in a part of the world that was so close to the United States, and he had issued an escalating series of demands that the junta step down. The three-man U.S. delegation had met with Cedras before, and they hoped to convince Cedras and his allies that their time in power had expired, and that Clinton was serious in his threat to invade the island nation in order to resolve the matter.

Though there had been much diplomacy and some blunt threats—Senator Nunn had reminded Cedras of a commander's duty to consider the welfare of his troops—there was initially no progress in obtaining a commitment from the junta. At 5:00 PM, Clinton ordered the U.S. military to invade Haiti, and told his envoys to leave the country. Carter relayed Clinton's order to Cedras and his officers in an attempt to convey the seriousness of the situation, but the Haitians were convinced that the United States would not act. "73% of Americans oppose an invasion," one Haitian officer said.

At that point, Haitian Army Chief of Staff Philippe Biamby entered the room holding a cellular telephone. "General Powell," he said, "the Americans have already launched, moved their paratroopers." A Haitian contact near

Fort Bragg in the United States had relayed to Biamby that the contact had seen the liftoff of the first of sixty-one planes that carried the 82nd Airborne Division en route to invade Haiti. It was this information, and not the blunt talk of experienced statesmen, that turned the tide. Only at that point did Cedras sign the agreement to step aside.

Here is an example of a crisis in which the threat to deploy the military was crucial to achieving a positive resolution, and a resolution without bloodshed on any side. It seems clear that the Haitian junta would have stayed in power absent a credible threat to remove them. Once the threat became imminent—the 82nd Airborne's planes were slightly over an hour from Haiti when they were ordered to return after Cedras conceded—only then were the Haitians' perspectives changed.

In this example, the military was critical to the peaceful resolution of the matter. However, it is not always the case that threats (and military activity in support of those threats) contribute to achieving the desired outcome. Sometimes, military measures can have an unintended and undesired impact.

Contrast Haiti in 1994 with events in Berlin in October 1961. Berlin had become a flashpoint in the Cold War. Soviet General Secretary Nikita Khrushchev had declared the isolated enclave of West Berlin a "thorn" in his side. On 4 June 1961, during Khrushchev's summit with President John F. Kennedy, Khrushchev issued an ultimatum: the Soviets would take measures to end the Western Allies' access to West Berlin by 31 December. Construction had begun on what would become the Berlin Wall earlier that year. Throughout 1961, tensions between NATO and the Soviets rose, to the point where Soviet and NATO tanks were squaring off against each other from either side of Checkpoint Charlie in Berlin.

During the crisis, General Lucius D. Clay (President Kennedy's personal representative in Berlin) ordered one of his subordinates to construct a scale replica of the Berlin Wall in order to find via experimentation the best way to breach the barrier, should it become necessary. The military goal was understandable: prepare for a possible confrontation. Washington countermanded the initiative when senior officials learned of it, but not before a section of wall had been built and bulldozers had been tested against it. Georg Schild argues that the Russians witnessed the wall-breaching exercise, claiming "Soviet military intelligence, probably through the East Germans, quickly learned of the construction and its purpose." One member of the U.S. Foreign Service at the time, informed of this dress rehearsal for an invasion, exclaimed "It's news to me!"

Here is an example of a military exercise that could have sent a signal to the Soviet Union that conflicted with the cautious diplomatic maneuvering being orchestrated from Washington. Had the Soviets considered this bulldozing experiment a credible indication that NATO military action was imminent, the result could have been an escalation of the crisis as a consequence of a U.S. military initiative that had not been ordered by the president. Though the October 1961 crisis was resolved peacefully, it serves as a warning of how military actions can potentially have an impact on crisis diplomacy that is opposite to the intention of the commander-in-chief.

United States presidents are granted a tremendous amount of latitude to manage a foreign policy crisis, in particular regarding military preparations and force deployments the president deems necessary. This is the longstanding interpretation of the commander-in-chief authority delegated to the president in the U.S. Constitution. The conduct of crisis diplomacy is largely uninfluenced by Congress and unfettered by U.S. law. At times, the movement of military material and personnel can alter the domestic political environment in which the possibility of foreign action is debated, and, perhaps most importantly, change the circumstances under which Congress will hold a vote on whether or not to authorize the use of military force.

Prior to the 1991 Persian Gulf War, George H. W. Bush sought Congressional authorization for the use of military force to reverse Iraq's occupation of Kuwait. Though many recall the Persian Gulf War primarily as a striking military success, the prospect of a major war to rescue a small and (to most Americans) unfamiliar nation was a contentious issue at the time. Some military analysts, such as Edward Luttwak, predicted a bloody conflict with U.S. casualties in the thousands. A Gallup poll conducted from 15–18 November 1990, found that 65% of respondents believed that the United States should not initiate a war with Iraq to liberate Kuwait. Though he was determined to reverse Iraq's occupation of Kuwait, Bush was concerned that he would fail to carry the day when Congress voted.

To prevent this, Bush altered the political debate over military action by sending hundreds of thousands of U.S. troops to Saudi Arabia in order to generate a credible offensive military option. By the time Congress voted on 12 January 1991 on the issue of whether to authorize Bush to employ military force to remove Iraqi forces from Kuwait, the administration "knew it would win" the vote in Congress. Many Democrats, including Senate Majority George Mitchell, did not want to be seen as undercutting Bush's last-minute diplomatic efforts by suggesting the nation was uncertain. Mitchell's view was not unique in Congress. For members of Congress, a vote to grant the president authorization to use military force can pave the way to later claim that one was voting yes in order to strengthen the president's hand in diplomatic efforts to avoid a conflict. Some argue that the media coverage of the January 1991 deliberation over the authorization of the use of force came too late in the debate, favoring those in Congress disposed to grant President Bush the authority.

Presidents enjoy wide latitude when responding to crises for two reasons. The first is the scope offered a president in the Constitution to conduct foreign affairs. The Constitution designates the holder of the office as sole controller of the nation's military—the "Commander in Chief of the Army and Navy of the United States." But what does this mean? Like so many aspects of the Constitution, the precise scope of this role is vague. In general, Congress has decided to interpret the president's commander-in-chief authority very broadly.

Second, and perhaps debatably, there is a political culture in the United States that promotes the idea that one should support the president during international confrontations. Though some presidential decisions to initiate or escalate crises have been unwise, rarely has a president found himself in a confrontation with an adversary who has not earned some measure of international condemnation. Congress may criticize presidential policy, but rarely does Congress actively obstruct a presidential position during a crisis. As Senator Trent Lott memorably phrased it during Senate debate over President Ronald Reagan's decision to deploy Marines to the Beirut airport in 1982, "We cannot have 535 prima donnas" advising the president on force deployments.

The moment of greatest tension during the Cold War was the Cuban Missile Crisis of 1962. This particular crisis is coupled with an unusually robust historical record, due to the fact that Kennedy taped most of the deliberations of the Executive Committee (EXCOMM) that advised him during the crisis. At times, while members of the administration deliberated the proper response, the military's actions or organizational culture obstructed the development of a full spectrum of options. The section below explores the 1962 crisis for insights into how the military's proclivities as an organization can potentially influence presidential decisions during a crisis.

The Cuban Missile Crisis

In October 1962, The United States and the USSR found themselves at the brink of a potentially apocalyptic confrontation. In defiance of multiple American warnings not to place offensive missiles in Cuba, Khrushchev decided to deploy surface-to-surface nuclear weapons and antiaircraft defenses in Cuba in May 1962. He was motivated, in part, by a recognition of the USSR's inferior ability to strike the United States from Soviet territory. At the time, the Soviets had only twenty inter-continental ballistic missiles

(ICBMs) capable of striking the United States. Deploying Soviet medium-range missiles to Cuba was seen as an inexpensive way of countering American superiority in strategic warheads. Khrushchev had hoped the missiles could be deployed and prepared in secret, but intelligence reports and U-2 aerial surveillance photography revealed indications of the Soviet operation before the missiles were ready for use.

Estimates of the number of people who could have been killed in a nuclear exchange between the two superpowers ran as high as two hundred million people. Once the crisis had been resolved, President John F. Kennedy privately estimated that the chance of a nuclear exchange was perhaps as high as 50%. Of course, Kennedy's estimate was not a scientific estimation of the true probability of a nuclear exchange between the two superpowers during those days in October. Nevertheless, given that Kennedy was one of the two key decision-makers involved in the crisis and was as well-informed as the entire Executive Branch apparatus could make him, his assessment carries weight. Kennedy and Khrushchev both were simultaneously horrified at the prospect of nuclear war and understood the need to project a willingness to risk vast destruction in order to obtain bargaining leverage.

For the purposes of explaining how the military's organizational culture can influence crisis deliberations, the Cuban Missile Crisis offers a number of examples of how organizational behavior affected the development of policy and the conduct of diplomacy with the Soviet Union. Specifically, there were a number of instances where the military's actions or organizational behavior operated contrary to Kennedy's will. Political scientists sometimes define this as irrational behavior—how the actions of a small part of a government can act contrary to the rational policy that the executive has selected. Three such examples are explored below.

One example involved America's nuclear alert posture which was signaled by a sequence of Defense Conditions, or DEFCONs. These Defense Conditions, created in October 1959, instructed U.S. forces worldwide on their designated state of combat readiness. The DEFCONs ranged from 1 to 5, with 1 indicating that all-out war was imminent.

On 24 October 1962, General Thomas Power, the Commander in Chief of Strategic Air Command, ordered the alert status raised from DEFCON 3 to DEFCON 2. Furthermore, he ordered that this instruction be sent uncoded or "in the clear," in order to be certain that the Soviets received an unmistakable signal that the United States had raised its alert status to a point just short of what would initiate a nuclear exchange. Here, then, is an example of a senior military officer taking the initiative, without higher approval, to send a highly significant signal to the other superpower—a signal that was not coordinated with the rest of U.S. policy. It was not inconceivable that Khrushchev and his advisors could have perceived the heightened alert status as the single determining indicator of hostile intent on the part of the Americans.

This example, then, suggests an alternative outcome for the crisis: an avoidable and catastrophic war between the superpowers. In a crisis with an old adversary, as preparations are made for combat on a global scale, measures taken by patriotic and well-intentioned senior leaders can disserve the aim of the president. A commander-in-chief must be alert to this potential.

A second example relates to the impact of organizational culture on officers' approaches to operational planning. During the early deliberations of the EXCOMM, some advisors initially came to the conclusion that a surprise attack on the missile sites was the only way to guarantee the Soviet missile threat in Cuba would be eliminated. General Maxwell Taylor, who had assumed the office of Chairman of the Joint Chiefs that same month, supported a confrontational response to the Soviet missile deployment.

In 1987, Taylor elaborated on why he initially favored the military option of destroying the Soviet missiles in a surprise attack:

> As an artilleryman, when I saw those missiles, with their transponder vehicles alongside of them, my immediate thought was they can pull them out and hide [them] any time they want to. And that was certainly the case. So if that's the case, and we announce to Khrushchev, 'We gotcha down there,' certainly at a minimum he'll hide those missiles in the jungles of Cuba, and we can never get [them] out unless we invade the island. Well, invading the island was the last thing I thought we should do, in our interest.[1]

This example illustrates how an officer's past military experience can cause him or her to focus on a particular aspect of a crisis, potentially obscuring more important elements that deserve greater consideration. Taylor's career as an artilleryman led him to focus on a particular facet of the situation— the mobility of the missiles. Seeing them not only as potential targets (as all participants in Kennedy's EXCOMM did) but, more specifically, as potentially elusive targets, he was concerned about how the Soviets would obstruct American efforts to target the missiles if Kennedy made a diplomatic overture or initiated a blockade.

In his 1972 memoir, with full knowledge of the crisis's outcome, Taylor pressed the advantages of the air strike option. "[I]t seemed essential to me to attack massively all known offensive weapons before they could fire," and also prevent them from being hidden. "[T]here was reason to hope that this demonstration of American determination . . . would bring Khrushchev to his senses and induce him to liquidate this rash venture." This last point is of interest, not least because Taylor recommended military action in part because he "felt that the quarantine alternative was more likely to develop into a choice between invading Cuba or backing down than was the *seemingly* more violent alternative of the air attack."

Even though he felt an invasion was "something the United States could not afford either politically or militarily," Taylor's earlier use of "seemingly" suggests an air attack was his preference. Yet Taylor hoped or even expected that Khrushchev would prefer to back down after a critical Soviet ally had been subjected to a surprise air attack. And this Soviet reversal would also occur after (in all likelihood) Russian military personnel had been killed in this bombing campaign. Taylor expects that the USSR will be strikingly docile and willing to retreat after a damaging surprise attack; the United States, in contrast, will feel compelled to escalate by the mere failure of a quarantine. This is a striking juxtaposition to say the least.

However, regarding his recommendation to attack from the air, was Taylor wrong? Not necessarily. This is an important aspect of decisions influenced by organizational behavior—the fact that one may be cognitively biased toward a particular conclusion does not necessarily mean that the conclusion in question is wrong. Regardless of whether Taylor was right or wrong, this example does point to one of the dangers of arriving at judgments based in part on one's organizational experience. Experience and organizational culture can bias an assessment in favor of a particular conclusion, potentially to the detriment of one's contribution to a national security decision.

By his own report, Taylor looked at the crisis from the first with the eyes of an artilleryman. This may have led him to be more in favor of military action than would have been a perfectly unbiased, coldly rational observer—an archetype which is, admittedly, hard to find in any presidential administration. Organizational culture can be pernicious at times, and a president would be foolish not to remain alert to this possibility, especially when one is being presented with possible courses of action during a crisis.

The third example from the Cuban Missile Crisis relates to the risk of inadvertent escalation. National Security Advisor McGeorge Bundy, in an interview long after the crisis, stated what he took to be one of its enduring lessons. "The most important thing about crisis management is not to have a crisis, because there's no telling what will happen once you're in one."

Kennedy expressed his fear of escalation on 29 October, leaving the horrible conclusion unstated:

> But my guess is, well, everybody sort of figures that, in extremis, that [sic] everybody would use nuclear weapons. The decision to use any kind of nuclear weapon, even the tactical ones, presents such a risk of it getting out of control so quickly.[2]

This is another risk that encumbers crises, especially crises of the scope and complexity of the Cuban Missile Crisis. Prior decisions establishing standard operating procedures and organizational design can influence perceptions of the best course of action. By the time a crisis has occurred, it is too late to reassess those decisions and recast one's operating procedures.

It should be noted that standard operating procedures are important military tools. Complex military operations would be impossible without some measure of pre-commitment to set routines. However, these routines come with unanticipated risks, risks that may become apparent only as the specifics of an individual crisis become clear. Consider the following exchange between Secretary of Defense Robert McNamara, and Chief of Naval Operations Admiral George Anderson:

> "When the ship reaches the line, how are you going to stop it?" McNamara asked the chief. . .
>
> "We'll hail it," the admiral said.
>
> "In what language—English or Russian?"
>
> "How the hell do I know? I have faith in my officers," said Anderson, his face glowing with anger. "This is none of your goddamn business. . . . We've been doing this ever since the days of John Paul Jones. If you'll just go back to your quarters, Mr. Secretary, we'll take care of this." He handed McNamara a copy of *The Manual of Navy Regulations*, saying "It's all in there!"
>
> "I don't give a damn what John Paul Jones would have done," said McNamara. "I want to know what you're going to do, now. What if they don't stop?"
>
> "We'll send a shot across the bow," said the admiral.
>
> "Then what, if that doesn't work?"
>
> "Then we'll fire into the rudder. . . . This is none of your goddamn business, Mr. Secretary. This is what we're here to do."[3]

This exchange offers an example of organizational behavior to the point of caricature. McNamara, understandably, wants to know if any of the pre-scripted Navy subroutines pose any risk of exacerbating tensions with the Soviet Union or, worse yet, leading directly to an unwanted and unanticipated escalation of the crisis. Anderson, though aware of the stakes involved in the confrontation, stoutly and coarsely resists what he sees as the Secretary of Defense's attempt to insert himself into matters of established naval practice.

Anderson himself is apparently unaware of what these procedures are in some instances. Although he knows that it is customary procedure to hail the ship one is intercepting, he is not only uninformed but also unconcerned about how this task will be executed. In his oral history interview with the Naval Historical Institute, Anderson presented a somewhat different version of the exchange, in which John Paul Jones was not mentioned. Still, he complained during his interview that the Navy relied on "standardized tactical publications" for all operations, and a commanding officer "has to follow it, and McNamara was getting into the instructions that these people had."

Crises and the Role of Reputation

In crises, there will often be political pressure to use or threaten to use military force to demonstrate the nation's resolve and commitment. In these circumstances, the military is a tool employed to maintain or bolster a nation's reputation for resolve.

While reputational considerations can be a concern, they can also be greatly overstated. In his book *Calculating Credibility*, Daryl Press offers examples of occasions when states estimated the likely reactions of their adversaries without reference to reputation, even in circumstances when it would appear that recent examples of vacillation during crises would be a major factor. He offers a theory, which he calls the "current calculus": "when leaders assess credibility in a crisis, they focus on the balance of capabilities and interests at stake in the current confrontation." These leaders will essentially ignore actions in recent crises, dismissing recent history as irrelevant.

Press chooses a tough set of cases against which to test his theory: the "appeasement" of Nazi Germany by Britain and France in 1938–9; Khrushchev's repeated failures to back up demands for a change in the status quo of Berlin from 1958–61; and the Soviet retreats prior to the Cuban Missile Crisis in 1962. These cases were selected because they involve a state weighing the demands of another state that had recently failed to follow through on a threat in a very public way. In essence, Press asked: "How does a state calculate the credibility of an adversary that has recently engaged in one or more high-profile retreats?" These should be easy tests for the theory that past actions matter when two states are engaging in crisis bargaining because the stakes were high, and the damaging actions that could have affected a state's credibility were quite recent.

Yet Press found that, in all three cases, retreats that should have led to a reputation for weakness did not lead to opponents' assumptions that future retreats would follow. Despite prior threats to the contrary, both France and Britain had acceded to the German annexation of part of Czechoslovakia by signing the Munich Agreement on 30 September 1938. If reputation played a role in calculating credibility, the two allies' reputations for standing firm in future military crises should have been poor, to say the least. Nevertheless, neither Hitler himself nor the German military reflected on the recent examples of French and British acquiescence in formulating their opinions of British or French willingness to fight over Poland and other matters. This is a success for Press's "current calculus"—Germany did not estimate France's and Britain's willingness to fight based on Paris and London's recent retreats, but instead relied on an estimation of the relative balance of capabilities and the relative importance of the stakes at issue.

Press applies his theory to another example, the Cuban Missile Crisis. Starting in 1958, Khrushchev had made repeated threats to end Western access to West Berlin. The United States, during both the administrations of Dwight Eisenhower and John F. Kennedy, ignored each of these demands and deadlines. Khrushchev failed to follow through on his own threats and did nothing. Despite Khrushchev's disinterest in following through on past threats, officials in the Kennedy administration did not weigh Khrushchev's prior retreats on the Berlin issue when they attempted to predict Soviet actions during the missile crisis. Instead, they calculated the relative importance of Cuba for the United States and the USSR—another success of the "current calculus" theory of state reputation in international crises.

This issue is an important one for understanding the proper use of the military in crises when reputational considerations play a role in national calculations. Often, presidents are criticized for not standing up to aggressive leaders, and for not responding to challenges with maximum toughness. President Obama, for example, offered an offhand reference to a "red line" regarding the use of chemical weapons in Syria, and then was criticized when he declined to respond militarily when evidence came to light that the Assad regime had used chemical weapons on Assad's own citizens in 2013.

While Americans are often fans of tough, resolute leaders, military action to maintain a reputation can be unwise and unnecessary—and often dangerous. A reputation for toughness is often of surprisingly little value in confrontations. For example, consider the highly credible U.S. threat to invade Iraq in 2003. Given the transparently aggressive bent of the American electorate in the post-9/11 environment, and the clear resolution demonstrated by President George W. Bush's deployment of an invasion force of 160,000 troops, there was no rational reason for Iraqis to disbelieve the seriousness of the threat. Yet, according to extensive post-invasion interviews with captured Iraqi officers, Saddam Hussein expected that the coalition would not risk significant casualties in a ground campaign. He remained in Iraq and was captured in December 2003, having declined opportunities to flee the country prior to the war. When facing the most credible threat of invasion in recent international history, Saddam did not believe President Bush's threat to fight all the way to Baghdad.

These examples bear keeping in mind when arguments are made about the need to fight to protect a reputation for toughness. One might ask: if one must always fight to protect a reputation for resolve, what, exactly, is the virtue of that reputation? Press concludes his volume with a stark recommendation: "countries should not fight wars for the sake of preserving their credibility."

Military Influence on Crisis Deliberations: The Persian Gulf War

The chain of command in the United States military is theoretically quite clear: the president gives orders, and those in uniform salute and execute those orders. That does not mean, however, that the ostensibly obedient officers at the president's command cannot influence the military decisions of the commander-in-chief. An astute general can subtly shape crisis deliberations. General Colin Powell offers us an example of an officer who was well positioned to have disproportionate influence on policy deliberations. A man well-versed in the ways of Washington, an officer who had experienced an unusually large share of postings to the nation's capital, and a former National Security Advisor, Powell had both a resume and a temperament that prepared him to utilize the formal and informal opportunities his office afforded to influence policy decisions.

After the Iraqi military seized control of Kuwait on 2 August 1990, President George H. W. Bush convened his national security team the following day. There was a broad consensus that Iraq's transparent violation of sovereignty must be challenged in some way. All of those in attendance agreed on the need to protect Saudi Arabia, and concurred with Powell's proposal that 100,000 troops be sent to the Saudi-Kuwaiti border as soon as possible. At this point, Bush made a promise: "We're committed to Saudi Arabia."

Powell posed a question: he "asked if it was worth going to war to liberate Kuwait." The question was not at all the casual inquiry it might seem. It was timed and framed in a way to set a tone for a debate over the wisdom of launching a war to remove the Iraqi military from Kuwait. For Secretary of Defense Dick Cheney and others in the room, it signaled unspoken reservations from the highest-ranking individual in the United States military. Following the meeting, Cheney felt sure that Powell "wasn't convinced" that Iraq's occupation of Kuwait was of strategic importance to the United States.

Powell was a politically astute individual—this was part of the reason he had been selected to be chairman over fourteen other four-star officers who had seniority over Powell at the time. Powell later admitted that he had spoken at this meeting in part as a response to his experience in Vietnam, when he "had been appalled at the docility of the Joint Chiefs of Staff, fighting the war in Vietnam without ever pressing the political leaders to lay out clear objectives for them." Before the military mobilized, he felt, someone had to ask, "to achieve what end?" The comparison to Vietnam suggests the scope of Powell's reservations at the time. Though he agreed with his critics on the National Security Council that he had overstepped, he did not regret his remark. Powell's intervention illustrates how a senior officer can seize an opportunity to influence a discussion—and, as in this case, a discussion that even the general himself believes may be customarily out-of-bounds for the military.

Unrealistic Expectations: The 2012 Benghazi Attack

The U.S. military is like any other large bureaucratic organization: it can be slow to respond to unanticipated situations. Certainly, it possesses units of varying size and deployment speeds that are intended for use in a crisis. The 82nd Airborne Division, for example, trains to be "wheels up" (airborne, en route to a target) eighteen hours after notification of the order to deploy. This is the largest rapid-response ground force in the U.S. military, requiring (in 2018) sixty-eight cargo aircraft to airlift the entire division and the equipment needed for a combat insertion.

However, an unanticipated event can strain or exceed the military's response capabilities, especially if it is of an unexpected scope and in a distant part of the world. This can lead to situations that vividly illustrate the limits of military power, and show how even the world's most expensive military can be a far cry from a global 911 police force.

The attack on the American diplomatic compound in Benghazi, Libya, on 11 September 2012 was one such event. Though there had been a smattering of low-level attacks throughout Libya, Ambassador Christopher Stevens and his team had no reason to expect a sudden attack on their compound by over eighty armed men. The military did have units in Europe that had been positioned for an emergency response, such as FAST units (Fleet Antiterrorism Security Team) stationed in Italy, but the bureaucratic apparatus had not been prepared for the rapid response that could have made a difference on that day in 2012. Consider the following excerpt from the House Panel investigating the attacks on the U.S. consulate in Benghazi in 2012, suggesting how difficult it is for even a defense secretary to muster the nation's resources in a crisis:

> By 7:00 p.m. in Washington [1:00 a.m. in Benghazi], nearly three hours after the attacks began, the Secretary issued what he believed, then and now, to be the only order needed to move the FAST platoons, the CIF [Commander's in Extremis Force, a unit under European Command], and the U.S. SOF [Special Operations Forces, also deployed to Europe]. Yet nearly two more hours elapsed before the Secretary's orders were relayed to those forces. Several more hours elapsed before any of those forces moved. During those crucial hours between the Secretary's order and the actual movement of forces, no one stood watch to steer the Defense Department's bureaucratic behemoth forward to ensure the Secretary's orders were carried out with the urgency demanded by the lives at stake in Benghazi. For much of the evening of September 11, principals in Washington D. C. considered Stevens to be missing and reliable information about his whereabouts was difficult to come by. For those on the ground and in the fight in Libya, the reality of a second American death was sinking in.[4]

The report written by a Republican-controlled House critiquing the response of a Democratic administration might be expected to be unforgiving. But the passage illustrates, from an operational standpoint, the limits of civilian command of the military. The attack was launched at approximately 9:42 PM Benghazi time. The best estimate of when Ambassador Christopher Stevens and Foreign Service Officer Sean Smith died of smoke inhalation is slightly after 10:00. By this timetable, any U.S. military quick-reaction force would have had to respond with sufficient force to repel several dozen armed occupiers of the compound within the space of approximately half an hour. Though the average American voter may believe that America's potent military should be able to protect American lives at a moment's notice, expecting a global response capability as fast as one's local 911 responders is far beyond the capabilities of even the U.S. military.

Notes

1 James G. Blight and David A. Welch, *On the Brink: Americans and Soviets Reexamine the Cuban Missile Crisis* (New York: Noonday Press, 1989), pp. 77–8.
2 Ernest R. May and Philip D. Zelikow, Eds., *The Kennedy Tapes: Inside the White House During the Cuban Missile Crisis* (Cambridge, MA: Belknap Press, 1997), p. 657.
3 Richard Reeves, *President Kennedy: Profile in Power* (New York: Simon and Schuster, 1993), p. 402.
4 United States House of Representatives, "Report of the Select Committee on the Events Surrounding the September 2012 Terrorist Attack in Benghazi," Part I, p. 89, 8 July 2016. http://benghazi.house.gov/NewInfo

5

THE DECISION FOR WAR

The Constitution grants the power to declare war to Congress. Writing in Federalist No. 69, Alexander Hamilton argued that the intent of this choice was to grant authority that would "amount to nothing more than the supreme command of the military and naval forces," and expressly make the position of President "inferior to that of either the monarch or the governor." As commander-in-chief, the president was to have only "occasional command" of the militia; the wartime role of the president was seen as "first General and admiral of the Confederacy." Powers that were seen as associated with the expansive role of a British monarch, such as the power to declare war and to raise and regulate military forces, were expressly given to Congress.

It is worth reflecting on the fact that the manner in which the Constitution addresses this critical presidential function could have been quite different. During the Constitutional Convention, it was briefly proposed that the Constitution give Congress the power to "make war," which could be interpreted to suggest that Congress play a larger role in the conduct of actual military campaigns, and not just the decision of whether or not to initiate hostilities. This could have led to a different approach to managing the nation's military during wartime—instead of giving the president vast latitude in his or her role as commander-in-chief, Congress could seek to insert itself into some portion of what are now considered presidential wartime decisions. But the language was changed to "declare war" following a floor motion at the Constitutional Convention, and the question was rendered moot.

How does the Constitution's direction that Congress is given the power to declare war impact the president's ability to use the military? This is a complicated question. One of the broader definitions of the president's war-making ability can be found in a government document stemming from the Iran-Contra Affair during the Ronald Reagan administration. In 1987, the House Select Committee investigating the Affair condemned the Reagan administration for evading appropriate Congressional oversight in illegally supplying arms to the Nicaraguan Contras using funds obtained by selling weapons to Iran. But the House minority report took a different view. It argued that the Constitution afforded presidents "some discretion to use military force without declaration of war," and suggested that the extent of this discretion "would have to be worked out in subsequent practice."

This is an expansive view of the president's war power. It suggests a pliable vision of the president's war-making ability, one that can be discovered by employment of that power. This minority report was specifically cited by Vice President Dick Cheney after 9/11, in that he thought it successfully presented "a robust view of the President's prerogative with respect to the conduct of especially foreign policy and national security matters." If effect, a highly influential individual in the George W. Bush administration was comfortable resting his interpretation of the scope of executive authority on a minority report from a House Select Committee written in 1987, and a committee report that had nothing to do with the struggle against terrorism.

Given that the authors of the Constitution clearly intended to give the power to declare war to Congress, one can rightfully ask: have successive generations done a good job of following this mandate? There is considerable room to argue that the Constitution's instructions regarding the initiation of wars have not been followed as the framers most likely intended. Congress has only rarely declared war in the nation's history. In only five of the nation's conflicts has Congress formally declared war, the most recent being the six separate declarations of war against the Axis and associated countries during World War II.

One of these five instances, the War of 1812, was highly unusual. In this conflict, a reluctant President James Madison signed a declaration of war on 18 June 1812, a declaration that had been pressed through by the "War Hawks" in Congress. Members of this Congressional faction were indignant at Britain's assertion of maritime rights and encouragement of Native American hostility. In effect, Madison had to be pushed toward war by political forces at home. In all other instances where the United States declared war on another nation, the president led the way and pressed for a declaration of war.

Many would argue Congress does not have the same level of responsibility for the security of the nation as the institution of the presidency. Congress was intended as the place where laws were debated, and as a check against the excesses of the Executive Branch. Some of the framers of the Constitution argued that a deliberative body was not the appropriate entity to grant final authority over the use of force. President John F. Kennedy later offered a Cold Warrior's perspective on why presidential independence from Congress in matters related to security was justified: "There's a big difference between a bill being defeated and the country being wiped out."

Congress attempted to reassert a measure of authority over the initiation of war following the conflict in Vietnam. The War Powers Resolution (WPR) of 1973 mandated that the president report to Congress within two days of committing U.S. forces to action, and it requires Congressional authorization for such deployments lasting longer than sixty days (with an additional thirty days allowed for the withdrawal of forces). When the resolution passed, Senator Jacob Javits of New York exclaimed, "At long last, Congress is determined to recapture the awesome power to make war." Others were more pessimistic. Senator Thomas Eagleton, one of the bill's original sponsors, came to doubt the efficacy of the result. He argued the resolution gave the president "a 60- to 90-day open-ended blank check" to take American forces into combat with no requirement to obtain authorization from Congress.

President Richard Nixon vetoed the resolution; Congress then passed it over Nixon's veto. Every president since Nixon, both Republican and Democrat, has questioned the constitutionality of the resolution and reserved for themselves the option of acting outside of it should the circumstances require. Richard Pious argues, "Presidents from Ford through Bush have routinely minimized, evaded or ignored its provisions, arguing that it is an unconstitutional infringement on their powers as commander-in-chief. . . . They ignore the prior consultation clause." When presidents do report to Congress in accordance with the Act, it is often in brief one- or two-page letters, each containing less information than could be found on a nightly news broadcast.

Even when presidents comply, they offer themselves great latitude to interpret restrictions on their commander-in-chief authority as they see fit. When President Reagan ostensibly acquiesced to the WPR by signing the Beirut Resolution in October 1983 (offering justification for the Marine deployment to Lebanon), he released a statement that undercut Congress's ability to set time limits on deployments. "[T]he initiation of isolated or infrequent acts of violence against United States armed forces does not necessarily constitute actual or imminent involvement in hostilities, even if casualties to those forces result." The president, of course, would determine the definition of "infrequent," and consequently would set the limits on when the WPR would apply.

There is no meaningful pressure from the public to alter this state of affairs. Americans grant considerable latitude to presidents when it comes to the use of force, since willingness to use force is often associated with strong leadership. In an exit poll conducted immediately following the 2016 presidential election, the highest percentage of respondents (36%) said that being a strong leader was the most important characteristic they considered when deciding whom to vote for. Second place went to "having a vision for the future" at 29%.

There are occasional efforts to reappraise the president's wide latitude to deploy the military as he or she sees fit. Particularly when a new president takes office, there may be efforts to press for reform of the process, sometimes led by high-profile national security figures. In 2007, James A. Baker III and Warren Christopher chaired the National War Powers Commission, a private appraisal of presidential war power empaneled by the Miller Center. The Commission issued a report the following year, calling for the War Powers Resolution to be replaced by legislation that offered greater specificity regarding the definition of hostilities and that required Congressional votes on deployments lasting more than thirty days, among other provisions.

However, these efforts generate only a small profile on the nation's political radar. Even in 2008, when an incoming President Barack Obama came into office having argued that presidential overreach lead to foreign policy disaster in Iraq, Baker's and Christopher's unusually prominent effort received little attention. Incoming presidents often shift their perspective on executive latitude in foreign affairs after they are elected. Once in office, presidential power that formerly seemed ripe for abuse can come to be seen as a potentially useful tool that cannot be safely set aside.

After all, a new president feels highly confident that he or she will be a responsible steward of the authorities of the office. Political allies may encourage them to adopt an expansive view of the scope of their powers, particularly when the nation faces a crisis. While President Franklin Roosevelt awaited inauguration and the prospect of global war loomed, prominent foreign affairs columnist Walter Lippman was comfortable telling the president-elect, "You may have no alternative but to assume dictatorial powers." This was an exchange that took place before the Japanese attack on Pearl Harbor.

Limitations on presidential war-making power can come from unexpected places. For even the most consequential of presidential decisions in this war-making realm—the decision to launch nuclear weapons—it is possible that consequential disagreements could emerge in a behind-the-scenes debate between a president and his most senior commanders. This potential fracture in presidential command and control of the military came to light early in the Donald Trump administration, during the intermittent tit-for-tat threats between Trump and North Korean President Kim Jong-un in 2017. There was speculation regarding whether Trump's threats, such as his offer to visit North Korea with "fire and fury" in August 2017, suggested that Trump was considering a nuclear strike to eliminate the prospect of Pyongyang pairing its known nuclear weapons capability with an evolving arsenal of long-range missiles capable of carrying atomic warheads.

General John Hyten, the commander of U.S. Strategic Command, was presented with an opportunity to shed some light on how the military might respond to a presidential order to launch a preventive nuclear strike. Speaking at a security conference in Nova Scotia in November 2017, Hyten replied, "We think about these things a lot." He then suggested that he would have no difficulty declining to follow an order he deemed to be illegal.

> And if it's illegal, guess what's going to happen? I'm going to say, 'Mr. President, that's illegal.' And guess what he's going to do? He's going to say, 'What would be legal?' And we'll come up with options, with a mix of capabilities to respond to whatever the situation is, and that's the way it works. It's not that complicated.[1]

This is a remarkable statement from a senior officer. A combatant commander is speculating, on the record, as to how he would decline a hypothetical order from a president, and explaining how he would then offer the president a range of alternatives. The statement suggests that Hyten has determined (or at least considered) what constitutes an illegal order, leading the listener to wonder as to whether he may have prepared his command to respond to and resist such an order. He even goes so far as to anticipate the president's response to Hyten's hypothetical demurral in what would be a situation of great tension. Perhaps Hyten's conclusions regarding this hypothetical scenario have been communicated to the president, in which case we have the strange circumstance of a commander telling a sitting president what orders he will or will not follow. Perhaps Hyten has kept his conclusions to himself, in which case the military is preparing to disobey a presidential order and publicly discussing how such disobedience could happen. Either circumstance is extremely unusual. Such statements from a senior commander probably do not strengthen the United States' hand vis a vis North Korea, nor are they likely to make the United States' nuclear deterrent seem more reliable to other potential adversaries around the globe.

It is worth emphasizing that even the statutory and Constitutional limits on presidential war-making authority are not self-enforcing. Congress's power to affect a President's ability to make war comes into play only when a significant number of members are disposed to prevent, curtail, or interrupt a presidential military initiative. Smaller military commitments, such as President Obama's decision to engage in Operation Odyssey Dawn in Libya, may elude robust scrutiny because too few members of Congress see the operation as meriting a full confrontation with the executive branch. In this case, Obama avoided the need to seek Congressional approval for the operation by ordering the Pentagon to fund the operation "out of hide," meaning using funds from elsewhere in the defense budget—to the consternation of then-Secretary of Defense Robert Gates. As of 3 June 2011, the Department of Defense's costs related to the operation (by one estimate) stood at $715.9 million. It speaks to the degree to which the nation's defense establishment is well-funded, that an operation costing several hundred million dollars can be paid for with the budgetary equivalent of "found money."

The Obama Administration—Three Cases

Consider three cases where a president who had criticized the office's expansive war powers—President Barack Obama—found himself making military decisions involving the use of force. First, in Libya, Obama confronted an unraveling state caught in the throes of the Arab Spring. Responding to what he believed was the threat of genocide in Benghazi and elsewhere, he relied on an 11 April 2011 memo written by Caroline Krass of the Office of Legal Counsel. While this memo did not cite unitary executive theory, it referred to the "independent authority" of the president in foreign policy. Interestingly, the memo also cited the inherent limitation of the sixty-day review period mandated in the War Powers Resolution, a limitation Obama later decided to set aside as the conflict dragged on. The letter also argued that airstrikes did not rise to the level of war, since no ground troops were involved—a definition of war that potentially allows for the aerial pulverization of an enemy without waging a "war."

The second case involved Syria. In 2013, Obama prepared to attack the government of Syrian President Bashar al-Assad, as a response to Assad's alleged use of chemical weapons in that country's ongoing civil war. Obama justified this action—an unprecedented military strike in response to the use of chemical weapons in another country—by again citing his latitude to act as commander-in-chief. 140 members of Congress, including twenty-one Democrats, signed a letter stating that action in Syria, under these conditions, would violate the Constitution. Secretary of State John Kerry said the president reserved the right to "respond as appropriate to protect the security of the nation." The attack on Syria never came to pass, as a diplomatic opportunity presented itself to negotiate Syria's surrender of its chemical weapons stockpiles. Here, again, Obama took an expansive view of the president's war-making capability.

The third case involved the Islamic State, or ISIS. Obama launched an irregular campaign to combat the organization starting in August 2014. As of this writing, the government believes that U.S. Air Force strikes have killed an estimated 50,000 ISIS fighters. Obama claimed authorization to conduct the campaign against ISIS under the 14 September 2001 Congressional Authorization for the Use of Force that was meant to target those responsible for the 9/11 attacks—despite the fact that ISIS as an organization did not exist on 9/11, but rather emerged following the United States invasion of Iraq in 2003. Here, again, is an example of a president affording himself the latitude to stretch definitions and authorizations to allow himself maximum latitude to act. Obama argued that ISIS was covered under the 2001 resolution because the group was "the true inheritor of Osama bin Laden's legacy—notwithstanding the recent public split between al Qaeda's senior leadership and ISIL."

Obama requested a Congressional authorization for the use of force against ISIS in February 2015, but Congress did not act. It is worth noting that the draft authorization sent by the Obama administration contained a provision that would lead it to expire after three years (unless reauthorized) and had a clause that revoked the 2002 authorization to invade Iraq. Why would Congress not leap at the chance to demonstrate its commitment in the fight against ISIS? After all, a CNN poll in September 2014 showed that few Americans would hesitate to endorse action against that unloved organization. The reasons for Congressional inaction on the president's request illustrates the unusual incentives at work on members of Congress as they consider voting on a policy matter.

First, at the time of the president's 2015 request, the U.S. military had already been engaged in the fight against ISIS for approximately six months. The issue of whether or not to use force against ISIS was largely moot. Members of Congress voting on the issue would get no accolades for authorizing a military operation that had been going on for half a year. Congress would, in effect, be trying to make an issue where most Americans did not perceive one to exist.

Second, how would the proposed authorization be phrased? Will the proposed authorization allow strikes against ISIS anywhere, at any time? That could be seen as overly broad. Should it specify only in Iraq and Syria? Even with this restriction, should any misfortune meet the U.S. effort in either country, a member of Congress who had voted to authorize Obama's use of force would be vulnerable to the charge that they endorsed a military blunder. For a member of Congress, a vote is a commitment. There is no reason to make a commitment for the record when the benefit is essentially nonexistent and the risk is very hard to predict.

If ground troops are sent and a messy occupation unfolds, should those members of Congress who voted for the act be blamed? The lessons of the vote to authorize force against Iraq have not been lost on any members of Congress. Those who voted to support the war—even if they felt that they were voting for the measure to enable the George W. Bush administration to conduct tough diplomacy toward Iraq—came to see that vote as an albatross, as the invasion led to an ill-conceived and bloody occupation.

Regarding the possibility of a vote to authorize military action against ISIS in 2014, members of each party had different concerns that led in the same direction of avoiding a vote. Democrats were wary of supporting a broad military effort, for fear of antagonizing their anti-war base. Yet a vote against military authorization would make those same Democrats vulnerable to the charge that they were ignoring ISIS's violent behavior. Republicans, in general, supported the effort, but had concerns about putting themselves in the position of having supported "the next Iraq war." These considerations contributed to Congress's decision to avoid what could have been an acrimonious and complicated debate over a broader authorization for the use of force against ISIS.

The lack of initiative by Congress in authorizing the fight against ISIS illustrates the profound disincentives facing that body in foreign affairs, even against a threat that is almost universally viewed as deserving of deadly force. Many members saw disadvantages to conducting a vote. It is far easier for Congress to quietly step aside and allow the president to take action. In doing so, individual members of Congress preserve maximum latitude for themselves to criticize Obama or any future president, while also dodging the issues that weigh on any attempt to compose even a brief, simple authorization of military force.

Of these three examples from the Obama administration—two involving military action and one involving a decision not to act—none are of the scope of a major war like Vietnam. Nevertheless, these cases support the argument that there is a pattern of Congressional inaction in foreign policy, and a tendency to leave the initiative with the Executive branch. Congress has been more assertive where Guantanamo detainees are concerned, passing laws that restrict the president's latitude to indefinitely detain those captured in the struggle against terrorism. Nevertheless, where the use of force is concerned, Congress has yet to engage in meaningful restrictions of a president's power.

Structure of Command

When a decision is made to go to war, the president deploys the needed forces through the established chain of command. The Goldwater-Nichols Act of 1986 established the Secretary of Defense as the office in control of all aspects of DoD functions. President Dwight Eisenhower had tried to impart this authority to the secretary's office by executive fiat in 1953, with only limited success. It took over three more decades for Congress to translate Eisenhower's wishes into law. As a consequence of Goldwater-Nichols, the defense secretary gives orders to the military on behalf of the president.

The primary military officer through which a president will command execution of military initiatives is the regional Combatant Commander (CCDR). This is a four-star officer responsible for all U.S. military involvement in that designated part of the world. The CCDR is responsible for contingency planning, supporting military-to-military engagement in the region, and the execution of military operations when necessary.[2]

This command structure—with a single four-star officer responsible for coordinating the efforts of all four services in any regional military effort—is in large part a response to difficulties encountered during World War II. In the European Theater of Operations, a single Supreme Commander, General Dwight Eisenhower, headed the Allied Expeditionary Force. Eisenhower acted in a manner that was similar to how regional CCDRs operate today. However, in the Pacific, the Army and the Navy had two separate commanders, General Douglas MacArthur for the Army and Admiral Chester Nimitz for the Navy.

Nimitz and MacArthur profoundly disagreed on core elements of the Pacific strategy. MacArthur favored an island-hopping campaign that would lead to retaking the Philippines. Nimitz thought it wiser to forego the islands and focus on Taiwan. Beyond these strategic matters, Nimitz and MacArthur held conflicting views on operational elements as well. Though the war in the Pacific was ultimately successful, the conflict between the two commanders was much on President Harry S. Truman's mind as the National Security Act of 1947 was being written. In Truman's words,

> We must never fight another war the way we fought the last two. I have the feeling that if the Army and Navy had fought our enemies as hard as they fought each other, the war would have ended much earlier.

Today, every regional CCDR has a broad range of responsibilities. Central Command's 2013 posture statement summed up the scope of the command's mission:

> With national and international partners, U.S. Central Command promotes cooperation among nations, responds to crises, and deters or defeats state and non-state aggression, and supports development and, when necessary, reconstruction in order to establish the conditions for regional security, stability, and prosperity.

For a commander responsible for most of the Middle East, this is a daunting charge, to say the least.

The United States is the only nation to divide the world into geographic areas of responsibility, with a senior military commander responsible for each region. The former Soviet Union is the only other country to have had a somewhat similar system, consisting of cones of responsibility radiating from Moscow. American CCDRs play a significant role in determining regional policy—they are often called to testify before Congress and even have independent opportunities to influence the procurement priorities of the Department of Defense. As Derek Reveron and Michelle Gavin note, "combatant commanders have a distinct advantage" over policymakers in the continental United States. The CCDRs "are forward deployed, have more flexibility than D. C.-based institutions, and have robust travel budgets." Consequently, the CCDRs play a major role in regional policy.

It should be emphasized that the Chairman of the Joint Chiefs, despite being the highest-ranking officer in the U.S. military and the chief military advisor to the president, is not in the chain of command at all. The chairman has many opportunities to influence the development and deployment of the force, and theater commanders preparing for a conflict will often consult with or defer to the wishes of the chairman. During the Persian Gulf War of 1991, theater commander General H. Norman Schwarzkopf spoke frequently to his chairman, General Colin Powell, as they prepared a strategy for evicting Iraqi forces from Kuwait. Nevertheless, orders to take military action are sent to geographic CCDRs directly from the defense secretary.

The chains of command for the use of force are clear-cut, and they are designed so there is no mistaking when an order or action has been duly authorized. But this is not to say that there are not times, especially during crises, when individuals operate outside of the scope of their authority. On 9/11, many of the highest-ranking members of government found it difficult to communicate with each other during the minutes and hours immediately following the attacks. At approximately 10:00 or 10:15 that morning, Vice President Dick Cheney was in the White House shelter conference room. A military aide informed him that there was an aircraft eighty miles away from Washington D. C., and asked for authority to shoot it down. Cheney gave the authorization. Despite the fact that the vice president is not the deputy commander-in-chief, the order was obeyed by the military as if it had come from the president. Later, both Cheney and President George W. Bush would claim that Cheney gave the order based on a prior conversation that morning with Bush.

The military's views on the wisdom of a proposed use of force have weight in policy debates. However, these factors may not affect the views of average Americans as much as one might think. One national survey of public opinion found that when the military supports a use of force abroad, this leads a 3% rise in the level of public support for that engagement. When the military is opposed to a deployment or use of force, the impact is more significant; the same survey found public support would see a drop of 7% if it were known that senior military officers had reservations about the operation. However, the actual impact of senior military officers having concerns about a proposed use of force would vary greatly based on how those officers expressed their reservations. There could be a profound difference in the political impact of a few remarks to a reporter off the record, and a decision by a CCDR to resign rather than execute an order.

Decisions regarding whether or not to lead the nation to war are the most significant a president can face. The framers of the Constitution envisioned that the assembled representatives in Congress would make such decisions. While Congress still plays a critical role in authorizing force where a major military commitment is at issue, presidential latitude to act independently increases as the scale and expected duration of the potential engagement declines. Americans tend to favor strong leadership in the face of what is often seen as an unstable world, and that support enhances the many advantages that presidents enjoy when they seek to confront foreign threats.

Notes

1 Kathryn Watson, "Top General Says He Would Resist 'Illegal' Nuke Order from Trump," *CBS News*, 18 November 2017.
2 For certain counterterrorism operations and other tasks, Special Operations Command will be tasked with the mission, instead of a regional CCDR.

6

STRATEGIC CHANGE IN WARTIME

In October 1862, after holding the presidency for seventeen months during the gravest crisis in the nation's history, Abraham Lincoln found himself a frustrated man. He had outfitted the Army of the Potomac, led by General George B. McClellan, with virtually everything McClellan had asked for. Following the battle of Antietam, Lincoln believed (correctly) that the rebel forces near McClellan's encampment were relatively vulnerable. But daily encouragement to attack from Lincoln, the ostensible commander-in-chief, had no impact on McClellan, who wrongly feared the Confederates were superior in number.

Lincoln was strolling near McClellan's vast encampment with a friend, Ozias M. Hatch. Cresting a hill, both men saw the endless lawn of tents that sheltered the one hundred thousand men of McClellan's force. Lincoln gestured, and asked "Hatch, Hatch, what is all this?"

"Why, Mr. Lincoln, this is the Army of the Potomac," Hatch replied.

"No, Hatch, no," Lincoln responded. "So it is called, but that is a mistake; it is only McClellan's bodyguard."[1]

At that moment, the president was simultaneously clothed in immense power and yet powerless; he was unable to command his commander.

Lincoln had endeavored to prepare himself to lead a nation at war. Early in the war, Lincoln recognized his lack of schooling in strategic affairs and had resolved to educate himself. He read Henry Halleck's *Elements of Military Art and Science*, a classic at the time. He frequently sought out updates from the field, especially when a battle was in progress. Lincoln even field-tested new rifle models himself. Eliot Cohen argues that the reason for Lincoln's success as a war leader goes beyond the fact that he continued his search for the right general longer than others might have. Cohen notes that Lincoln was willing to involve himself in any aspect of the war and its specific operations. Today, Lincoln's degree of engagement in the Army's operations might be criticized as micromanagement of the military. This mode of leadership is certainly on the opposite end of the spectrum from how other presidents, such as George W. Bush, handled similar pressures.

Nor was Lincoln shy in using the president's ability to fire a general at will. Lincoln went through seven commanding generals over the course of a war that lasted just less than four years, a pace of change in top military leadership unrivaled by any modern wartime president. Over the course of the eight-year Iraq war, from March 2003 to December 2011, no commanding generals were relieved prematurely for battlefield failure, and this despite the fact that there were periods during the Iraq conflict when most thought the occupation was going poorly.

There are no military decisions that are outside the purview of a president; the title of commander-in-chief carries with it the office of micromanager-in-chief. In political discourse, a president may dismiss a decision as being too "operational," as if there are military decisions that a politician cannot or must not address. In reality, this means that the politician in question is either uncomfortable with the operational decision in question, or is disinterested in that aspect of an operation or conflict. That disinterest may well be appropriate for the situation at hand. Even within the military chain of command, delegation of authority is critical to any operation.

President George W. Bush was particularly comfortable defending decisions by saying he was following the recommendations of his commanders in the field. Sometimes Bush's deference involved decisions of consequence, such as whether or not to send in thousands of reinforcements. In April 2008, as his administration debated the options for U.S. strategy in Iraq, Bush told Gates "I've told him [Petraeus] he'll have all the time he needs." The political advantage to such a stance is that it saddles a president's detractors with the yoke of being "against what the military is asking for." Even a president's most vigorous opponents are not eager to don the mantle of denying requests from troops in the field.

When a president contemplates a change in strategy during wartime, there are two psychological proclivities he or she should bear in mind. First, military leaders are understandably disposed to seek a path toward victory. Generals are not trained how to lose a war. When a military effort seems at risk of leading to failure, there can be intense pressures to find a way to use the vast resources of the United States to snatch victory from looming defeat. This is a recurring conundrum for the United States military and those who lead it. Escalation is often an option for a resource-rich country like the United States, but an increase in effort does not always lead to a winning endgame, as America's slow defeat in Vietnam reminds us. Indulging in the course of "trying harder" can come at the cost of additional lives lost in a doomed pursuit of victory.

Second, the knowledge that one's fellow citizens have died in pursuit of victory can spur the living to see promise in a renewed effort where perhaps no promise exists. Lincoln's Gettysburg Address memorably asked Americans "to be dedicated here to the unfinished work which they who fought here have thus far so nobly advanced" and admonished "that these dead shall not have died in vain." Policies acquire a terrible human gravity once lives have been sacrificed to achieve the aim in question. While such sacrifice demands respect, presidents must strive to keep in mind that sacrifice does not require spending more lives to extend a failing policy. Lives lost do not mitigate the heavy onus placed on a president to make the correct decision, even if it means commanding a retreat or admitting failure.

Obama's Afghanistan Surge

During a speech at West Point in December 2009, President Barack Obama announced one of the more controversial strategic shifts of his presidency. He had decided that an additional 30,000 U.S. troops would be sent to Afghanistan, in what he believed was a final effort to set that country on a different and more stable path. While the troop increase was deliberated for months, Obama's senior leaders (both civilian and in uniform) sought ways to steer the decision toward what the force commander, General Stanley McChrystal, had requested: an additional 40,000 troops. This case study offers an example of how public military advice can constrain a president's latitude to determine the best course of action.

Recognizing the importance of the first major strategic decision of his presidency, Obama took many months to consider the available options. The outcome of the deliberation was uncertain; some senior officials, such as Vice President Joe Biden, advocated for a gradual and complete withdrawal from Afghanistan. In this uncertain environment, Obama's senior generals began some unsubtle lobbying for a larger increase. Generals David Petraeus (the CENTCOM commander) and McChrystal gave interviews in late 2009 that made the case for a troop increase. McChrystal's August 2009 "Commander's Assessment" had concluded that the international force deployed to

Afghanistan "required more forces." The report was leaked to the media in September. Clearly, having the commander's assessment in the public realm puts a president in an awkward position. As Obama's Chief of Staff Rahm Emanuel put it, "Between the chairman [Admiral Michael Mullen] and Petraeus, everyone's come out and publicly endorsed the notion of more troops. The president hasn't even had a chance!"

Vice President Biden worked out a plan with the Vice Chairman of the Joint Chiefs, General James Cartwright, that called for 20,000 troops, about half of what McChrystal and Mullen wanted. Mullen saw to it that the 20,000 option received little attention. After some internal discussion and a brief and superficial war-game "test" of the 20,000 option at the Pentagon, it was essentially shelved. However, Obama sensed that he was being prodded toward the higher troop increase. During a November national security meeting to review options in Afghanistan, Obama told Mullen that he felt he had been given essentially only one option to consider. "That's unacceptable," the president said. Though Mullen agreed with Obama's assessment that the Joint Staff "owed" Obama additional military options, his staff never provided them. Obama ultimately decided on an increase of 30,000 troops.

The Afghanistan surge was met with disfavor by many Democrats who would normally have preferred to support Obama. Democratic skepticism of the surge led to a rare example of significant Congressional pressure on a president to alter a military policy. In July 2010, 153 Democrats in the House cast votes to require the president to offer a clear timetable for bringing the conflict in Afghanistan to a close. Even Speaker of the House Nancy Pelosi joined this overt criticism of Obama's approach to troop levels. It marked a rare example of Congress seeking to insert itself into an arena that is normally the sole purview of the executive branch. The proposed Afghanistan withdrawal timetable failed in Congress, in large part because of Republican votes against it—Republican votes in support of a Democratic president. Secretary of Defense Robert Gates later conceded that his officers had promoted an overly optimistic view of the prospects of success, such as McChrystal's suggestion that there was an Afghan "government in a box" ready to hit the ground running when Afghanistan's Helmand province was stabilized. Although Obama sent almost as many troops as his commanders had requested, the optimistic projections of his senior officers did not come to pass. By the time Obama left office, Afghanistan was far from stable. The change in strategy that Obama's military leadership had endorsed was a failure.

Even a president who begins his or her term in office unfamiliar with the domain of military affairs must recognize the possibility that only the individual in the position of president has the maximum latitude to impose a strategic change when change is needed. As Ted Sorenson argued in 1963, presidents must be prepared to use the full scope of their powers:

> [A] president cannot afford to be modest. No one sits where he sits or knows all that he knows. No one else has the power to lead, to inspire, or to restrain the Congress and the country. If he fails to lead, no one leads.[2]

Powell During the Persian Gulf War

As an example of how a seasoned and politically astute general can steer his or her commander-in-chief toward a desired strategic change, consider Powell's influence on strategic decisions prior to the 1991 Persian Gulf War. Chapter 4 examined how Powell had tried to make certain that the policy process weighed the relative merits of a war to liberate Kuwait. This section examines how Powell steered the administration's deliberation over war strategy.

When considering Powell's career, it is worth keeping in mind that the position of Chairman of the Joint Chiefs had only recently been made the independent and empowered position we now understand it to be. The Goldwater-Nichols Act of 1986 had been in force for three years when Powell became chairman in October 1989. The inaugural post-Goldwater-Nichols chairman, Admiral William Crowe, had consciously recognized the need to "go slow" in utilizing the new powers of the chairmanship, so as not to antagonize the previously dominant chiefs of staff of the individual military services. Powell would benefit from Crowe's approach, and then demonstrate the new powers of his position.

On 2 August 1990, Iraqi forces invaded neighboring Kuwait and rapidly seized control of the entire country. President George H.W. Bush built a broad international coalition that sought to reverse Iraq's annexation of Kuwait. We now view the outcome of the Gulf War as a textbook combination of astute strategy and dominant military capability. However, from the standpoint of the development of the strategy, it is important to recall the reservations many Americans had over the war. When asked if Bush should quickly begin military action or wait and see if sanctions forced an Iraqi withdrawal, large majorities of those polled (70–80%) between 23 August and 18 November felt that the U.S. should wait and see if sanctions were effective. The military buildup was slow. After Iraq's invasion, five months elapsed before the United States-led coalition launched its attack on 17 January 1991. The lengthy buildup took a considerable political toll, and suggested to some at the time that the United States was an impotent superpower.

During this time, there were predictions from Edward Luttwak and others that a ground campaign could lead to thousands of U.S. casualties. At the same time, there was pressure to employ America's superior air power for a quick result. President Bush himself told Powell, "Colin, these guys have never been seriously bombed," implying that a merciless and demoralizing air campaign alone could achieve the desired strategic result. This pressure to launch an air campaign continued for weeks and weeks. There were, in short, any number of incentives and opportunities for Powell to decide to be a more pliant general and support the idea of relying on an air campaign.

Instead, Powell not only sought to prepare for a ground campaign, but to do whatever he could to maximize the force at the coalition's disposal. In October 1990, when Schwarzkopf requested that Powell allow him to return from Riyadh to brief the president on military options, Powell asked that Schwarzkopf remain in Saudi Arabia. Powell then coached the briefers Schwarzkopf sent, coaxing them not to oversell the air power element of the plan. Bush, on multiple occasions, asked about the possibility of waging war with air power alone. Powell always countered along the lines of what he said during an NSC meeting on 30 October: "Mr. President, I wish to God that I could assure you that air power alone could do it, but you can't take that chance." This is a remarkably direct recommendation from a general to a president.

The force Powell requested was large, even larger than what Central Command had requested. At the end of October 1990, Powell asked President Bush for an additional Army corps, a doubling of the number of deployed Marines, three more aircraft carriers (bringing the total to six), and nearly a doubling of the number of Air Force planes. Bush agreed to all of it. After the war, Bush admitted that some thought the troop request was excessive, but he did not want to be accused of shortchanging the military. "The important thing was to be able to get the job done without leaks about divided views [within the administration] on force requirements." One wonders if Powell anticipated this reaction, and if this led him to believe he could successfully request the maximum.

With his maneuvering, Powell had had a considerable influence on the shift to a robust ground option. No member of the cabinet was pressing for as large a force as what Powell recommended. Indeed, National Security Advisor Brent Scowcroft (a general himself) gasped when he heard the size of Powell's troop request and wondered if Powell was trying to dissuade the president from action by daunting him with a large force. Deputy National

Security Advisor Robert Gates was of a similar mind. Powell later insisted, "I was not gaming him. Anybody who had the ability to generate overwhelming force should do so."

Schwarzkopf might have been of a similar mind regarding the desirability of a large ground force, but it is doubtful that the general nicknamed "Stormin' Norman" would have been able to steer high-level deliberations as adroitly as Powell did. Other generals who lacked Powell's gifts for timing and nuance found their efforts to steer U.S. strategy ended in failure. On 16 September 1990, the *Washington Post* reported on an interview with Air Force Chief of Staff Michael Dugan. In addition to revealing some detail about a potential strategy for an air campaign, Dugan stated, "airpower is the only answer that's available to our country." There is some evidence that Dugan was particularly eager to wage such a campaign. He had ordered subordinates contact recent Iraqi defectors and exiles in an attempt to compile an up-to-date list of potential targets. Dugan was soon dismissed for publicly revealing operational plans.

Powell's strategic advice was borne out by events, and the 1991 Persian Gulf War was heralded as the "100 Hour Victory." However, a general with a bad plan in mind could certainly use the same strategies Powell employed. A senior officer is often well-versed in the arts of shaping a briefing, preventing alternative plans from being thoroughly considered, and steering a leader's cognitive process toward a desired outcome.

Trump: Steered Toward Escalations in Afghanistan

Early in his administration, President Donald Trump found himself subjected to similar pressure from his senior national security aides. Trump had been dismissive of the goal of nation-building at times before taking office. During the Obama administration, Trump had tweeted his perspective that money spent on Afghanistan was being wasted, and that those taxpayer dollars would be better spent at home. Once in office, he occasionally expressed doubt about the course of the conflict in Afghanistan. "We're losing," he said on 19 July 2017, during a meeting in the White House situation room. "What does success look like?"

However, when he announced his future Afghanistan strategy on 21 August 2017, he had decided on an escalation of America's effort in Afghanistan. According to early accounts, Trump's reservations about staying in Afghanistan had been worn down by debates with three members of his national security staff, all of whom were serving officers or retired military: Defense Secretary James Mattis, National Security Adviser H. R. McMaster, and Chief of Staff John Kelly.

These three men had steadily bombarded the president with images of the bleakest possible repercussions of a withdrawal. The Taliban would be resurgent and potentially take control of the country. There would be more incidents like the May 2017 truck bomb in Kabul that killed 150 people. Afghanistan could become a haven for the Islamic State. There appear to have been no influential members of the cabinet voicing the arguments in favor of withdrawal, as Vice President Biden had been during the Obama administration. Steve Bannon, a senior adviser to the president, had offered reservations about the United States' trajectory in Afghanistan, but he was fired shortly before the change in Afghanistan strategy was announced.

With a national security team heavily weighted with military men, there are reasons to expect that the debate would avoid the uncertainties of withdrawal and stay with the known, if unhappy, status quo. The military does not train officers on how or when to exit a conflict. Military service is a vocation that drives its followers to achieve what appears unachievable, even at the gravest personal risk. As Mattis himself said of service members, "We're almost hard-wired to say 'can-do'. . . . That is the way we are brought up, routinely, and in combat, that is exactly what you do even at the risk of your troops and equipment and all." Staying the course can be a courageous and wise decision at times, but a president must be sure that his or her military advisers recommend steadfastness out of wisdom, and not due solely to a loathing of defeat.

Notes

1 Matthew Moten, *Presidents and Their Generals: An American History of Command in War* (Cambridge, MA: Harvard University Press, 2014), p. 125.
2 Theodore C. Sorenson, *Decision-Making in the White House: The Olive Branch or the Arrows* (New York: Columbia University Press, 1963), p. 83.

7

THE TASK OF POSTWAR RECONSTRUCTION

When a war ends, the soldiers return home.

Few wars truly end this way, but for most modern societies in most conflicts, there is at least a broadly-held aspiration, if not an expectation, that the grinding and deadly task of combat should most naturally give way to a conclusion of the military's role. The soldiers have endured the searing task of battle. They, more than any, have earned the quiet healing of peace.

Sadly, what has been earned is not always received. Depending on the course of the conflict, the military can become deeply involved in postwar efforts to engage in political stabilization, economic development, counterinsurgency, and deterrence of third parties. Wars are not tidy, and neither are their conclusions. One conflict that could have defied this pattern was the 1991 Persian Gulf War, which appeared to offer the potential for a neat and brisk ending. The U.S.-led coalition had the sole military aim of liberating Kuwait and sought no long-term occupation of Iraqi territory. Nevertheless, the United States established two no-fly zones (in which aircraft were intermittently downed during the following decade) and maintained a regional military presence.

After the end of a war, a president still makes consequential decisions regarding military actions. The most consequential of these decisions is whether to impose a political transition on a defeated foe, and if so, how to go about it. The United States is in the habit of asking military service personnel to undertake reconstructions of U.S.-occupied states, largely due to the lack of a capable alternative to the Department of Defense. Even presidents who were dubious of the wisdom of nation-building efforts have felt compelled to order the military to undertake exactly this task. During the 2000 presidential campaign, George W. Bush said, "Are we going to have some kind of a nation-building corps from America? Absolutely not." That maxim crumbled after 11 September 2001.

A recent and relevant example of a postwar reconstruction effort was the U.S. military's struggle to manage political transition in post-invasion Iraq. The toll of this effort amply illustrates the importance of presidential decisions following the invasion and overthrow of the Ba'athist government. While over 4,400 U.S. service personnel were killed during the course of the invasion and reconstruction, only 138 Americans died during the invasion itself. This means that over 97% of the U.S. military deaths in Iraq came after the invasion was successfully concluded. For both Americans and Iraqis, the end of Saddam Hussein's regime marked the beginning of their peril.

Iraq's reconstruction was also a large-scale and politically prominent policy initiative, one conducted in the post-9/11 environment—a time when spending large sums of money on anything related to national security was unremarkable, even popular. However, the Iraq effort became politically contentious as it wore on, and there were opponents in Congress who wanted to use the power of the purse to shut down the entire enterprise. Members considered using one of the awkward but potentially potent tools at its disposal for matters related to national security: the ability to deny funding. In April 2007, at the nadir of public support for the war, Senate Majority Leader Harry Reid endorsed a measure to cut off funding by 31 March 2008. "It is not worth another drop of American blood in Iraq," Reid said. That Congressional initiative failed, as did others. No politician relishes the prospect of being in a position where she or he can be accused of not supporting the troops.

Why did Iraqi civil society disintegrate after 2003? The proximate causes are easily suggested, such as the dismantling of the Iraqi military and the bureaucracy. Andrew Flibbert argues that the conduct of the war inadvertently attacked the infrastructure of the state itself. Aside from the Ministry of Oil, the coalition military effort targeted every Iraqi state apparatus. Paul Bremer's "Order No. 1" of 16 May 2003 cast tens of thousands of Ba'athists out of the government. These and other measures effectively collapsed the Iraqi state and "opened to contestation the most basic questions of political life. . . . States are easier to break than to make, even for the dominant actor in a unipolar world."

Robert Gates, as he prepared to leave the office of Secretary of Defense in February 2011, offered a telling warning of America's limited capabilities in this regard:

> In my opinion, any future defense secretary who advises the president to again send a big American land army into Asia or into the Middle

East or Africa should 'have his head examined,' as General MacArthur so delicately put it.

For any president contemplating the military's potential role in a postwar environment, it is important to grasp the obstacles that the military faces when dealing with complicated social reconstruction efforts. The remainder of this chapter addresses some of the prominent caveats that such a presidential decision should take into account.

Reconstructing a nation is a complex social task, to say the least. Maximizing the probability of success demands a deep understanding of a nation's society, culture, language, and politics. As if that assignment were not daunting enough, one must also assess the short- and medium-term trajectories of each of those factors. Those trajectories may be radically different from the nation's recent history, and they will be ineluctably and profoundly influenced by the recently concluded conflict. From the perspective of a skeptic, the task is a nightmare, even for a brigade of social scientists.

A president must approach this sort of endeavor with a realistic appraisal of the military's capabilities in this regard. American service personnel will address any task to the best of their ability, and will seek out the appropriate expertise. However, there is a gulf between military training and full-spectrum preparation for engaging with a foreign society. Consider the account of ill-preparedness for civil policing from Larry Diamond, who was a senior advisor during the earliest days of Iraq's Coalition Provisional Authority:

> We needed to fill, much more quickly, the vacuum of conventional policing. In a country the size of Iraq, international actors must deploy thousands of 'armed international police to monitor, train, mentor, and even substitute for indigenous forces until the creation of a proficient domestic police force,' according to a RAND study published shortly after the war. We had no ready reserve of specialists in rebuilding civilian policing after the conflict.[1]

Reconstruction efforts require surge capacities that are not aligned with the primary foci of the U.S. military. Though cultural indoctrination for service personnel being deployed to Iraq improved within a few years of the start of the occupation, initial attempts to prepare U.S. service personnel for their immersion in Iraqi society were rudimentary. Some of the first American troops deployed to support the reconstruction received a four-hour briefing on Iraqi culture and a short booklet of social do's and don'ts. Translators, at least, were in plentiful supply, but a good translator is not a substitute for experience interacting with the society in question. For Secretary of Defense Donald Rumsfeld, engaging the social science community was not seen as a priority, partly due to concerns that civilian academics would be politically biased against the Bush administration. It is also true that some academic organizations, such as the American Anthropological Association, attempted to prevent their members from assisting with the reconstruction.

Religion is another factor complicating social reconstruction efforts, one that has been misunderstood by military officers and U.S. officials involved in recent efforts. In post-invasion Iraq, the Coalition Provisional Authority (CPA) initially did a poor job of understanding the role of Shia religious figures in the country. Some senior officials, such as Deputy Secretary of Defense Paul Wolfowitz, believed that Iraqis would embrace secularism after Saddam Hussein was overthrown. Iraqi exiles advising U.S. government officials downplayed the role of Grand Ayatollah Al-Sayyid Ali al-Husseini al-Sistani in Iraqi society.

Consequently, when Sistani issued a *fatwa* (a religious edict) in June 2003 calling for only elected representatives to rewrite Iraq's constitution, the head of the CPA—Paul Bremer—tried to ignore Sistani's decree. Bremer soon found that both Iraqi politicians and other Shi'ite clerics deferred to Sistani, and as a result, Bremer was unable to enact his plan for replacing Iraq's constitution without a direct election. The CPA had expected Sistani would remain aloof from politics, since he had announced that he was not interested in running for office. The Americans failed to grasp that clerics could remain outside the political system and still have great influence over Iraqi politicians.

Another complicating factor in reconstruction efforts is the challenge of selecting appropriate and accurate measures of success. In war, the measures of physical success on the battlefield—number of miles advanced; number of enemy tanks destroyed—are often concretely observable. One knows when the military is succeeding in combat because one can chart progress on the battlefield, and estimate the number of enemy units that have been rendered ineffective. Assessing progress in a reconstruction effort is a different task. It involves selecting and assessing a range of complex metrics, instead of gauging whether an objective has been taken.

This is why the military, when engaged in reconstruction efforts in Afghanistan and Iraq, often tried to shift the media's focus to physical achievements—a school was built here; a well was dug there. I have repeatedly had military officers in seminars who have expressed dismay (and, at times, anger) that the American and international media failed to report their unit's contributions to the reconstruction of Iraq or Afghanistan, and instead covered only incidents of violence and acts of resistance. Though the officer in question may be deeply familiar with the impact a new school had on a particular community, that school may be largely irrelevant from a broader development perspective. It is true that the media can be biased in the direction of reporting violence ("if it bleeds, it leads"), but it is also true that violent acts may speak more tellingly of the problems encumbering a reconstruction effort.

When success does occur, it may be caused by factors other than military measures. Consider the Iraqi surge ordered by President George W. Bush in January 2007, in support of which Bush ordered over 20,000 additional troops to be sent to Iraq. The surge followed significant changes in strategy ordered by General David Petraeus, who shifted the focus of U.S. forces in Iraq to protecting the population and building relationships. The period of the surge was followed by substantial declines in civil violence in Iraq, leading many to credit Bush and Petraeus with having successfully found a way to dramatically reduce the level of civil conflict.

Some argue, however, that the real reason for the success was more complicated. There was a dramatic shift in Sunni attitudes toward the insurgency between 2004 and 2007. This was partly due to changes in how U.S. forces interacted with the Iraqis, but also due to changes in the media environment. Iraqi media became more diversified, as competitors to al Jazeera multiplied and carried a message that was more sympathetic to the U.S.-led occupation. By 2006, some jihadists in Iraq were complaining that they were losing the media war. Iraqi Sunnis contributed to this perception. As part of the Sunni "Awakening," Iraqi leaders publicized al Qaeda massacres in the country, pointing out how these violated Iraqi norms and killed innocent civilians. There was also a change in Iraqis' perception of the likely outcome of continued civil conflict. Iraqi Sunnis realized they would not triumph over the Shia in a sectarian war, and this realization changed their perception of the U.S. role.

As Marc Lynch puts it, "It is important to see how deeply the Awakening violated the prevailing Arab normative consensus, the insurgency's discourse, and Iraqi tradition." This, Lynch argues, was the critical additional element that lead to the success of Bush's surge, an element that the U.S. military benefited from but did not initiate and could not control. The U.S. military was a critical factor in the success of the surge, but absent the independent actions of Sunni communities, the tale of the surge in Iraq would be a different story. In addition to knowing how to measure success, it is important to know the causes of success as well.

The military plays a major role in gauging the success of any initiative it is involved in, including reconstruction efforts. Initially, it plays the primary role, since critical information regarding whether an individual operation was successful or not is often based on information from the military itself. This raises a clear tension that must be kept in mind—the same organization that executes a campaign also has a major voice in determining whether that effort is gauged to be successful or unsuccessful. This does not mean that the military intentionally misleads the public, but there is still the organizational impulse to put a positive light on the military's actions, and at times to color the description of an outcome while still adhering to the truth.

The length of military tours in theater can also have an impact on reconstruction efforts. Army tours of duty during the occupation of Iraq tended to last approximately one year. Tours for the other services tended to be shorter: nine months for the Navy and Marines, often six to nine months (though sometimes twelve) for the Air Force. There were periods when the length of tours could be extended, particularly as the insurgency was accelerating from 2006–07. For example, in 2006, Secretary of Defense Donald Rumsfeld extended the 172nd Stryker Brigade Combat Team's time in Iraq by four months. In general, the Army has preferred to have an active duty unit deployed for no more than one year out of every three. Longer periods of deployment can lead to political problems, as extended tours are often followed by complaints from family members back home. As a spokeswoman for the Military Families Association put it, "Once you are talking about the second birthday missed, the second anniversary missed, it becomes very hard."

This system leads to problems in a reconstruction effort. When the force's focus is combat operations, it is feasible (though certainly not easy) to cycle units in and out of theater. Combat skills can be replaced. For reconstruction efforts, however, acclimating to a specific cultural environment and local conditions takes time and skill. Relationships with local officials are forged over the course of a tour, and those relationships are not always transferable. The need to bring troops home for rest and recovery, while essential for a unit's well-being, can hamper a reconstruction effort.

I interviewed an Army officer with four tours in Iraq who claimed that Iraqi insurgents were aware of the rotation schedules of American units, and would "wait out" coalition troops until they were scheduled to depart an area. While operational details such as rotation schedules are not public knowledge, neither are they secret, and it is not hard to get a private to divulge when the unit is departing. The Army officer I spoke to argued, "much as I hated long deployments, the way to win [to successfully reconstruct the country] is to do it like we did in the European Theater during World War II—you stay there until the war is won." Though the World War II approach would have cured the problem of fractures in the reconstruction effort during unit transitions, it was not remotely feasible with today's military and was never considered.

Nation-building can seem deceptively plausible at the outset. In the eyes of an American, the country in question should *want* to be reconstructed. Who would not prefer to be a citizen in a wealthy, prosperous democracy, a friend of the West set on a path toward future success? Who would not want to throw off the yoke of tyranny and be more like the United States? This common psychological trait, sometimes called mirror imaging, involves assuming that a member of a different society wants the same thing that you expect you would want in their position. This assumption can be profoundly inaccurate.

However, it is true that the United States can point to successful reconstruction efforts in its history. Nazi Germany and Imperial Japan were made into democratic states that became stalwart postwar allies of the United States. For some George W. Bush administration officials, the task of reforming Japan and Germany seemed more difficult than the task of reforming Afghanistan or Iraq. If the United States succeeded in those efforts following World War II, why not try the same approach with Afghanistan and Iraq? Reconstructing countries that are smaller and less dangerous than the Axis powers should be less daunting than the nation-building that followed World War II, they reasoned.

This comparison, however, overlooks a number of dissimilarities. A critical difference is that Germany and Japan were sophisticated, industrialized nations prior to the start of World War II. They were largely ethnically homogeneous (especially Japan), and their populations were eager to set aside the devastation of war. While the Japanese had fought the Allies bitterly and relentlessly during the war, and at great national sacrifice, postwar Japanese society sought to repair and renew the nation. John Dower titled his Pulitzer Prize-winning assessment of postwar Japan *Embracing Defeat*, capturing the essence of Japan's postwar perspective in two words. Dower later assessed the factors that contributed to Japan's reimagining of itself:

> Discipline, moral legitimacy, well-defined and well-articulated objectives, a clear chain of command, tolerance and flexibility in policy formulation and implementation, confidence in the ability of the state to act constructively, the ability to operate abroad free of partisan politics back home, and the existence of a stable, resilient, sophisticated civil society on the receiving end of occupation policies —these political and civic virtues helped make it possible to move decisively during the brief window of a few years when defeated Japan itself was in flux and most receptive to radical change.[2]

Neither post-invasion Afghanistan nor post-invasion Iraq displayed the qualities Dower identified in 1945 Japan that contributed to the latter's postwar stabilization and reconstruction. Afghans and Iraqis did not recognize the American occupiers as legitimate. Neither Afghans nor Iraqis had formed a strong concept of national unity. In Iraq, sectarian fractures soon came to dominate domestic politics. For Afghanistan, the idea of nation (as opposed to tribal loyalty) was, for most citizens, a foreign notion, and neither country had a recent history of economic vitality. Afghanistan in particular remains one of the world's poorest countries.

State reconstruction may be the most complicated social task that humans can undertake. In some instances, nation-building is more complicated than the preceding war. Combat deployments can be planned in advance and combat maneuvers can be drilled, but reconstruction efforts cannot easily be rehearsed. Even in a well-planned reconstruction effort, errors will occur. As former Secretary of Defense Robert Gates put it, "No matter how skilled and professional the U.S. military was, I knew that some abusive or insulting behavior by troops was inevitable." This concern could be applied more broadly to reconstruction efforts: mistakes will be made, potentially catastrophic ones. Presidents contemplating the necessity of reconstruction efforts would do well to consider the military's limitations in this regard.

Notes

1 Larry Diamond, *Squandered Victory* (New York: Owl Books, 2006), p. 306.
2 John W. Dower, *Cultures of War* (New York: W.W. Norton, 2011), p. 338.

CONCLUSION

> If we desire to avoid insult, we must be able to repel it; if we desire to secure peace, one of the most powerful instruments of our rising prosperity, it must be known, is that we are at all times ready for war.
>
> —George Washington[1]

Let me reiterate a point made in the introduction. This book has not attempted an evenhanded, comprehensive assessment of how the military contributes to American national security. Instead, it has focused on the facets of the military that could present problems for an American president who is attempting to do his or her best to secure the United States without overreacting to threats, without wasting taxpayer dollars, and without unnecessarily fueling crises and conflicts.

In effect, this volume has attempted to look at the military in a manner similar to how the military looks at the world: as a complicated environment that is to be scanned for worst-case scenarios. The military is staffed by millions of dedicated, intelligent, experienced, and patriotic individuals. However, one does not need much familiarity with international history or organizational behavior to realize that the collective result of well-minded individuals within a large and complex organization can lead to a result that ultimately disserves the nation's interests. Limitations on a president's time and attention, the military's ability to influence domestic debates and avoid presidential guidance, and the vagaries of the political winds all conspire to limit a president's capacity to impose his or her will. As Scott James reminds us, "Presidents confront a yawning gulf between the duties of their office and the inadequate formal powers at their command."

In Federalist No. 23, Alexander Hamilton wrote of his vision for presidential control of the military:

> The authorities essential to the care of the common defense are these—to raise armies—to build and equip fleets—to prescribe rules for the government of both—to direct their operations—to provide for their support. These powers ought to exist without limitation: Because it is impossible to foresee or define the extent and variety of national exigencies, or the correspondent extent and variety of the means which may be necessary to satisfy them.

Hamilton's vision was one of considerable latitude for the president. In contrast to the constitutional framers' concerns with limiting a president's domestic powers, Hamilton felt comfortable arguing that the president's control over the military "ought to exist without limitation." He was certainly correct when he reminded his fellow citizens that it would be impossible for any of them to predict the full spectrum of national security challenges that would face future leaders of the democracy they founded.

By the time two centuries had passed since the Constitution was signed, the United States had constructed—partly out of necessity, partly out of desire—a military apparatus that vastly exceeded any force that Hamilton or his contemporaries could have imagined. In addition, advances in military technology have created contingencies Hamilton and his contemporaries could not have anticipated. The advent of nuclear weapons forced the institution of the presidency to be prepared to make a decision of cataclysmic consequence for the globe, and to make that decision in a time frame measured in minutes instead of weeks.

Though the United States continues to prepare for large-scale conflicts of the sort that defined the twentieth century, those wars appear increasingly unlikely in the twenty-first century. Limited conflicts against weaker powers, such as those that have defined the administrations of George W. Bush and Barack Obama, are the most likely conflicts the United States military will encounter in the post-9/11 era. Congress has, to date, offered support at the initiation of these conflicts and is close to powerless while they are waged. It is still true that a president is not free to deploy the military at will, but against a plausible threat and in the face of a perceived need, Congress is likely to avoid confrontation with the Executive Branch over a limited deployment of the military.

As has been discussed, the nation's most senior military officers may blur the line between soldier and policymaker at times. Clausewitz observed,

> At the highest level the art of war turns into policy. . . . This assertion that a major military development, or the plan for one, should be a matter for purely military opinion is unacceptable and can be damaging. Nor indeed is it sensible to summon soldiers, as many governments do when they are planning a war, and ask them for purely military advice.[2]

Active duty senior officers can have an impact on the political environment as well. In 2009, General David Petraeus (then the commander of Central Command) gave scheduled testimony to Congress. Petraeus largely offered a standard assessment of the status of his region, but a single paragraph of his statement addressed the repercussions of the Israeli-Palestinian dispute on U.S. security interests. Petraeus argued:

> Israeli-Palestinian tensions often flare into violence and large-scale armed confrontations. The conflict foments anti-American sentiments due to a perception of U.S. favoritism for Israel. Arab anger over the Palestinian question limits the strength and depth of U.S. partnerships with the governments and peoples of the AOR [area of responsibility] and weakens the legitimacy of moderate regimes in the Arab world. Meanwhile, al-Qaeda and other militant groups exploit that anger to mobilize support.[3]

This brief section of Petraeus' remarks garnered a considerable amount of attention, since military officers only rarely stray into politics and policy.[4] This points to a significant aspect of the military's role in political debates: the most senior officers rarely speak on political matters, but when they do, their words can have a disproportionate impact on the debate.

During his tenure as Chairman of the Joint Chiefs, Colin Powell engaged in an even more overt political intervention, one against the sitting president's wishes. Early in his tenure, President Bill Clinton decided to repeal the policy of not allowing homosexuals to serve openly in the military.[5] Powell was deeply opposed to allowing homosexuals to openly serve and went public with his opposition. "This is a judgment that will have to be made by political leaders," Powell observed. But he added "the military leaders in the armed forces . . . continue to believe strongly that the presence of homosexuals within the armed forces would be prejudicial to good order and discipline." Clinton decided he was not well positioned to overcome the resistance he faced, even though he could have ordered the military to comply. The president relented to the general.

Robert Gates offered an unusual insight into the role of the presidency. Gates noted with admiration that President Barack Obama recognized that his cabinet secretaries and key advisors would not always keep him fully informed. Obama confided to Gates that the president was occasionally troubled by the possibility that important information was being kept from him:

> He concluded with what I thought was a very insightful observation twelve days into his presidency: 'What I know concerns me. What I don't know concerns me even more. What people aren't telling me worries me the most.' It takes many officials in Washington years to figure that out; some never do.[6]

There is a reason the largest and most complicated national organization in a country is often its military. The scope of the task of engaging in a modern war, the complexity of that endeavor in a technology-driven international environment, and the timeliness with which a modern military must be prepared to respond to a national emergency, all conspire to demand an institution of size and capability. It is an investment made in the hope that it will never be needed. To serve the nation that elected them, presidents must strive to understand the institution of the military, its strengths, and its proclivities.

Notes

1 George Washington, "Fifth Annual Message to Congress," 3 December 1793.
2 Carl von Clausewitz, *On War*, edited and translated by Michael Howard and Peter Paret (Princeton, NJ: Princeton University Press, 1976), p. 120.
3 Cited in Dennis Ross, *Doomed to Succeed: The U.S.-Israel Relationship from Truman to Obama* (New York: Farrar, Straus and Giroux, 2015), p. 348.
4 The Obama White House claimed the general had cleared his remarks.
5 The ban was not contained in U.S. law at the time, and therefore could be overturned by presidential order.
6 Robert M. Gates, *Duty: Memoirs of a Secretary at War* (New York: Alfred A. Knopf, 2014), p. 300.